Principles of Truth

bj King

1st WORLD
PUBLISHING

Principles of Truth

bj King

Copyright © 2025 by bj King

Published by 1st World Publishing
P.O. Box 2211, Fairfield, Iowa 52556
tel: 641-209-5000 • fax: 866-440-5234
web: www.1stworldpublishing.com

First Edition

ISBN Softcover: 978-1-4218-3596-9

LCCN: Library of Congress Cataloging-in-Publication Data

What I offer to you in this book are my own opinions and beliefs based on direct experiences with Spirit over the past forty years and information I've consolidated from reading Ancient Wisdom teachings. These statements are not presented as THE TRUTH. Do not accept what I have written as truth only as one person's opinion. Accept only what resonates with your own discernment, your own truth. Discernment is one of the spiritual gifts promised to us all. If you do not feel you have it, pray for it. All spiritual gifts are given to us as a result of our asking for them. How you utilize the information in this book you do at your own risk, I accept no responsibility.

Table of Contents

1.

Who Are You And What On Earth Are You Doing Here?

We are not our bodies. We are not our egos. We are Spirits, aspects of much larger Oversouls, who have chosen to deliberately come to Earth for this Human experience. We have chosen to come to bring certain vibrations to Earth and Humanity. We have come to experience being encased in the density of physical bodies and then to wake up and remember we are not our bodies. We are spiritual beings choosing to have Human experiences. We are each a spark of God, this individuated spark causes our hearts to beat. Everything and everyone is an aspect of God. We feel fear, when we forget this, when we believe we are separate from God. We have come to Earth to allow our Oversouls, larger aspects of God, to work through these bodies for the benefit of Earth, all species of life on the Earth and beyond. These beings who are not presently in Human bodies are concerned with what is happening with Earth and Humanity, because everything that happens on the Earth affects everything and everyone in the galaxy, the Universe and beyond, because it is all God. Our mission is to remember and to consciously evolve toward reunification with God (Source) through awareness.

Past generations of souls have come to Earth intending to bring the message, Humanity was destined to progress by sharing and comparing knowledge. Yet, once here, it is easy to forget who we are and the mission. It is easy to succumb to fear, to believe we are the bodies and to forget to use our intuition. It is easy to develop a conscious or unconscious need to conquer, to dominate and to impose our needs and desires upon others and the Earth, because we have forgotten the truth, of who we are and why we are here. We develop an addictive identification with our bodies, as who we are and listen to our egos rather than our Spirits. The ego's only job was to keep the body alive so the soul may operate through it. We have given over much more control to the ego than is productive to the accomplishment of the mission.

When we believe it is purposeful enough to just survive and build a better, more secure World, for our children and ourselves, we enter the mass consciousness trance, the World of illusion. We expect to be "saved" by the government or the return of a Messiah from what we have collectively created through our thoughts of fear and by forgetting who we truly are.

We are not here to discover our place in the economy, to survive and to find meaning in family and children. We are not here just to live well and to create a more secure World for succeeding generations. We are here to allow our souls to participate through us, remembering our divinity, the divinity of all beings. We are here to promote unification.

There is no one who is unimportant to God. Each of us were created to give expression to the Divinity within us through our personal gifts. There are no unimportant jobs. Sharing our gifts with the World is our purpose, no matter what our job description might be or what our written resume says about us. We are here to minister to human hearts. If we talk with anyone, see anyone, or even think of anyone, with love, then we have the opportunity to bring more love into the World. We are on Earth to experience love and wonder. Once we understand this, we can understand that if we focus our attention on loving ourselves, loving the Earth and loving all other creatures, we will experience abundant lives. True abundance and peace do not come from focusing on money, they come when we focus on love, peace, wonder and acceptance.

> *"To love what you do and feel that it matters—*
> *how could anything be more fun?"*
> — **Katharine Graham**

We have all had and may still have "a job" or we can choose to have "a calling or a mission." You can make any job you have your "calling or mission" if you understand your purpose is to be love, be God doing that particular thing, through you, for the benefit of Earth and all Humanity. Even if we have a job for survival reasons we can make it into a "mission" a "calling", because wherever you are is where your soul has called you to be at this time.

The soul has a purpose for wanting your body to be in that place, at that time, with those particular people. If we stay aware and acknowledge the great mystery that is life, we will see we have been perfectly placed, in exactly the right position...to make all the difference in someone's World.

That doesn't mean you have to stay in a job or relationship you do not enjoy, but it does mean there is a purpose. Be grateful for the job or relationship you have and design the one you prefer. The sooner we identify the purpose, define (write it down) and choose another future, the sooner the soul will co-create that future with us.

For each of us there is a personal dream waiting to be discovered and fulfilled. We are to dream our dream, invest it with love, creative energy, passion and perseverance. Intuitions, dreams and coincidences are all designed by our souls to keep us on the path to discovering and fulfilling our dream, the dream of the soul. Our job is to pay attention and to follow the clues.

If you could work in any setting, what would it be? What are your ideal working hours? Imagine your ideal workplace surroundings. What do you see? Compare your ideal with what you are experiencing currently. Are there any similarities? What one thing can you change that would make what you are currently doing closer to your ideal? This applies even if you are retired or so wealthy you do not need to work for money.

We each need to understand our heart's desires so we can live the soul's desires. We cannot make our daily choices in favor of our heart's desires until we identify those desires. Our life always changes in one of three ways, through crisis, chance or choice. The life we are now living is a result of the previous choices we have made. To have a better life only requires making wiser choices.

Little choices are important.
In fact little ones can often be more life-altering than big ones.

Make a conscious choice every day to shed the old: old fears, old issues, old guilt, old limiting beliefs, old patterns or habits of eating, drinking or smoking, patterns of responding or not responding, patterns of suppressing anger or resentments or expressing them in inappropriate ways. The old need to compete or to resent the success of others.

What are three small choices or changes you could make now, to begin to enhance your life in big ways? Eat less, drink less, smoke less, talk less, listen more, take a daily walk, write a singles ad or reply to one, spend less, read more, write the first draft of a novel or your life story, paint a picture, turn off the television, visit a friend, write a letter, tell someone you love them, smile more, draw the plans for your dream home, begin to trust your instincts, begin to listen to your soul.

We are here to experience joy. If we are not in a state of joy it is because we have unforgiven aspects within our sub-conscious and conscious minds. The path to joy is through forgiveness, first forgiving ourselves and then forgiving all others as if they are ourselves. In actuality we have called them into our lives to point out some part of ourselves we have not forgiven. Forgive yourself if you have forgotten your divinity. Ask the Holy Spirit to assist you to forgive.

Ask for the Divine Plan of your life to unfold through joy.

Being alive as a Human, but not remembering why you are here can be very depressing and anxiety producing. Once you agree to remember why you agreed to come to Earth at this particular time, a great sense of adventure can be born within you. Humanity as a whole is evolving toward remembering everything we knew in the afterlife and to make this knowledge conscious on the Earth. If we make that our goal individually – to remember—we become part of the solution, rather than part of the problems happening on Earth.

When we are born into the physical we run into the problem of going unconscious and through being trained or socialized into the mass conscious reality. We forget where we came from and why we came. We succumb to the Fear. Then hopefully we awaken one day and question, can this be all there is? Surly there is more to life than this struggle. There are beings from our Oversouls observing us. Watching for us to wake up, waiting for us to ask this question. They are constantly beaming energy into the illusion we have created here on Earth, hoping to wake us up. When a person begins to question, why am I here? Who am I really? Their intuition will increase due to additional amounts of energy the Oversoul will begin to send into the physical body.

Regardless of the behavior we observe in others the truth is all Humans are attempting to wake up to the truth of their being, their divinity. The more positive energy we give to them, the better the chances are they will wake up. When we see someone behaving in a controlling, uncon-scious, vicious or violent manner sending them the energy of disapproval, judgment and condemnation only adds to their confusion and gives more negative energy to be acted out. When we see someone suffering in this way, be they our boss, spouse, a politician, a child or a terrorist, we have a responsibility to focus on their divinity not on their action.

I allow Spirit to teach classes, through me, and often I take dowsing rods and measure the energy of a volunteer person's aura, which will usually be radiating about three to six inches from their body. When I back up and tell them I am going to hold a positive thought about them and once again approach their body their aura is much larger. I then ask them to hold a negative thought about themselves and I approach their body again and once again their aura will register almost non-existent. When the whole class focuses positive or negative energy toward the candidate their aura will expand and contract in relationship to the type of thoughts being projected toward them. If we project negative thoughts toward a politician, who is making decisions affecting large portions of Humanity and the World, we are adding to the problem and not creating a positive space around them in which they could wake up and make positive decisions. We can send anyone positive energy by focusing on the spark of Light in their heart and expanding it, without agreeing with their philosophy. To anyone we see operating in a challenging way we can mentally say, "Bless your heart." Then we become a part of the solution.

We have deliberately chosen this physical life experience at this time. Knowing why we have chosen to be here, and what we had planned to accomplish or learn, will enhance our experience of our lives. One of the most deliberate choices we made was to come to Earth to co-create a life of joyful productivity. We came to remember we are not just physical, but are also energetic, magnetic and spiritual. We chose to come to Earth to remember we create our reality by the power of thought, intention, and emotion.

We can choose to be deliberate co-creators or creators by default. Creation by default happens when we are not clear about our intentions and we let our thoughts run wild without any control or conscious recognition of what we are thinking. The majority of people on the planet today are creating by default. They set forth thoughts; they attract creation; they do not understand they have done it, so they blame or credit someone else. If we learn to co-create consciously and deliberately we can have easy, healthy, joy-filled lives.

Many people have become numb to their life experience, because of tuning in to mass consciousness beliefs and what they are exposed to through the news media and television. Exposure to the mass media can cause a person, who is not strong enough to think for themselves, to feel hopeless. Watching the media can cause a person to begin to shut down their feeling nature in order not to be negatively affected by the violent scenes they witness on the news and in movies. After watching so many buildings and people explode, a person's perspective of what is real diminishes. Violence begins to be acceptable to the sub-conscious. The feeling nature shuts down. The line between what is real and what is fictitious is blurred. It is important to your spiritual nature and your purpose of coming to Earth not to expose yourself to violence and acts against Humanity. Our feelings connect us to our soul communication. When we numb our feelings, by subjecting ourselves to violence, we lessen the possibility of direct soul communication.

To avoid seeing the violence of the newscasts is not sticking our heads in the sand to pretend these things are not happening. It is more difficult to hold a positive thought for and about Humanity if we expose ourselves to the anger and violence displayed as news or entertainment.

Our purpose is to hold the thought of what we desire for ourselves and Humanity.

When we think of something destructive we add energy to destruction. When we see something that offends us, like the killing of whales and dolphins, it is not helpful to be "against" the killing of whales and dolphins. We are to never go to war against what we don't want. Only being in favor of what we do desire will change the outcome. If we think of what we don't want, because of the Universal Law of Attraction, we give energy to it. Only by being in favor of peace will peace happen.

Being "anti war" does not create peace. Being against World hunger doesn't feed people; only by being in favor of every person on Earth being housed, clothed and fed will it happen. Having a "war on drugs" doesn't stop drug traffic or stop the reason people use drugs. Only by being in favor of every person being addiction free and having strong self esteem will we cause the outcome we desire. Focusing our thoughts and emotions on what we don't want brings more of what we don't want. This is the Universal Law of Attraction.

It is easy to get caught up in the conversations of those around us and their emotions. This is particularly true when the people we are with begin to complain about our government or government officials. We cannot change the behavior of government officials by complaining about their beliefs and actions. We can only change their actions by focusing on what we desire their actions to be, how we desire them to behave. If we expect them to act in controlling fashions, if we expect them to be dishonest, greedy, self-serving, they will be. Through thoughts and emotions others can stimulate our thoughts and emotions in directions that are not positive for us. Just as effectively we can stimulate positive thoughts and emotions in others by focusing our intention and thinking positive thoughts about them. It is important to hold clear thoughts and emotions relating to what we desire to have as our experience and the experience we desire to see for the World and Humanity. If we do this we can hold our beliefs, thoughts and emotions regardless of what is going on around us. But if we accept what we see or hear is "how it is" and we feel helpless to change it, because of course we are only one person, then the people who appear to be in charge will continue to behave in obscene and self-serving ways. Until we are strong in our desires, of how we desire to feel and what we desire to have as our experience, it is important not to subject ourselves to those who hold and express negative thoughts and emotions. We are too easily caught up in their beliefs of reality. Our reality is what we make it, through our thoughts.

We came to Earth to experience the beauty of Earth and to experience interaction with other Humans, plants, minerals and animals in a loving positive manner. We came to make a positive contribution to the expansion of spiritual energy, beauty and love on the planet. We came to remember we are not just physical, but are spiritual beings having a Human experience. We came to remember that we are connected to a soul that is much larger and more powerful than the body we inhabit. What is in the body is not all of who we are. We did not come to just exist or to survive. We came to thrive, to co-create, to self-actualize.

We are here to self-actualize, which means to become all we are capable of becoming. We can accomplish this by connecting deliberately to our souls in order to be reminded by our souls why we came to Earth and what agenda we had before incarnating. Why did we choose these particular parents? So we could learn how we didn't want to be as adults or did we choose people who are stellar examples of parenthood? We chose the race, the parents, and the country for a reason. We wanted to learn. **We are to never stop learning.** We are to always be aware of what we are thinking and why. What we are thinking and feeling are our greatest guides to what we will create. **What we have thought and felt in the past is what has built the life we are currently living.** If we don't like some aspect of the life we are living, we can change the way we think and feel about that aspect, by beginning to focus on what would correct this aspect of our lives.

We came to Earth to bring Spirit into matter. Every Human being intended, prior to this physical birth, to come into physical form. We intended to deliberately create, by using our conscious thinking minds. We intended to remember we are spiritual and physical beings. We came to Earth, at this time, because when we were in Spirit, we realized this time in Earth and Human evolution there would be tremendous energy for co-creation and growth.

The energy that causes our hearts to beat is spiritual energy. The beating of our heart is our connection to our soul. Scientists have been unable to prove the source of this energy. They do know it is electrical, but they also know it is more than electrical. Physicians can use electric paddles to restart a person's heart that has stopped beating, but it will not work every time. If it is time for that person to transcend the physical, no amount of electrical stimulation will be able to make their heart continue to beat.

We do not learn from words. We learn from experience. Words can stimulate thought, which creates action, which creates experience. Until we have experienced a thing we cannot truly "know" it. We send out thoughts. These thoughts create life experiences. Through these life experiences, we begin to "know" what we desire and what we do not wish to continue to experience. Even though we have lived before it is a blessing that we do not remember our previous lives. Not knowing enables us to consciously remain focused on this lifetime and that which we wish to accomplish in this lifetime without distraction.

The soul, the part of us that transcends physical birth and death, does remember all of the lifetimes we have experienced both physically and in the non-physical. <u>The purpose of each life is spiritual growth</u>. The soul realizes physical life provides great opportunity for soul growth. The soul knows we are the creators of all that occurs in our life experience. It is time for us to realize this truth and to begin to operate consciously, to manifest the experiences we desire, rather than to manifest by default.

2.

Every Thought Has Creative Power

When we focus on what we don't want to happen, we give energy to that happening. When we focus on the lack of something we desire, we attract more lack, rather than what we desire. In order to have what we desire, we must focus our thoughts and emotions on that which we desire with intention. Every thought is not equal in its ability to create. The more emotion behind a thought the faster the event will become physical. Therefore it is important to realize if we fear or dread something we are calling that event to ourselves. Repetition of thought, "habitual thought" causes creation even if there is not great emotion behind the thought. This is why it is important to look at our "habitual" thoughts. What thoughts run through our minds when we are driving, showering, shaving, putting on our makeup? What thoughts do we have when we are not deliberately thinking?

We usually repetitiously think "I want" or "I need?" If so, the sub-conscious mind takes our thoughts literally and believes we desire to stay in a state of wanting or needing, since that is what we are asking for. It is important to think literally, since the sub-conscious takes our thoughts literally and works to manifest what we are thinking and imagining. Therefore it would be more prudent to think "I desire, intend, deserve and now gratefully accept," rather than to think need, want or to think about what we lack. This statement fulfills the rules of manifestation: desire, belief, gratitude, expectation or anticipation. We often think we are ready to have something, such as a relationship, when in actuality we have conflicting emotions and thoughts about how having a relationship would change our lives. Being ready to accept, what you ask for, is extremely important. If we ask for something and it appears in our lives, but appears through a source we don't want to receive from or through, we can deny the manifestation believing God does not know the best way for us to get what we are asking for. It is useful at the bottom of each page of writing out your intentions to place this affirmation:

"I now accept this or something better, through the grace of God and to the highest good of all concerned."

We do not always know what is to our highest good. We don't always think big enough or expansive enough. We don't always understand why a certain person would be sent to help or to serve us. If we use this affirmation we can trust that the situations we manifest will be "win/win" for all parties concerned.

It is important to have dominant intentions about our lives. If it is our dominant intention to be healthy, wealthy, wise and to have mental and emotional clarity at all times, we are much more likely to have a happy life than if we are filled with doubt, fear, guilt, jealousy and greed. It is also important not to get caught up in trying to figure out the "how" a thing could or will happen. In doing this we have a tendency to miss create. Leave the "how" to God.

3.

My Personal Experiences With Manifestation

RELATIONSHIPS

My first marriage I was nineteen. I married a young man from my graduating class. It took me four and a half years to realize he was gay.

I met my second husband the night I moved out from my first husband. It became obvious, through the years, he was planted in my life by my soul. I was married to him for fourteen years, the marriage produced two children, who I later learned were the reincarnation of his parents, who had died when he was a junior in high school. I left him after fourteen years to marry an Episcopal priest. He was also a plant, brought to me by my soul, to draw me away from my lifestyle in Texas. He died, in my bed, of a heart attack four days after I moved to join him. I was devastated and the last thing I wanted was to get involved with another man, but of course the soul had another agenda.

I went back into banking, which was the only profession I knew. I attended a seminar on bank teller security and developed a relationship with the instructor. When he left Oklahoma, to move to Houston to take another job, he suggested the people who offered the class from Oklahoma University to hire me to teach the class all over Oklahoma. They never asked me about my degrees or education they just hired me on his belief I could do it. I had always been shy and had never spoken before a group of people. I got used to speaking to groups about being a bank teller, which was something I knew and understood. It was the soul's way of getting me into public speaking. I later heard from my soul, "God does not choose the

17

qualified. He qualifies those who choose to serve." This has certainly been my experience in being able to paint, write and teach.

About a year later I was taking dance lessons and met a man who was an executive in banking. Meeting him led to my becoming a bank consultant for a large savings and loan association. It was a time when savings and loans were shifting to become banks. My relationship with the man only lasted a few months and he married someone half my age, while we were still seeing each other. It became obvious later the job was why he had come into my life.

The next relationship was also planted by my soul. I had given up the idea of being in a relationship. My choice to follow my soul's guidance and my children were more important to me than romance. I met a man through Silva Mind Control, in a meditation class, who I thought could be with someone like me, who could know things before they happen and could know things about other people. The soul insisted I ask him to marry me. I thought because he had been involved in metaphysics for fifteen years that he could live with a psychic comfortably. Nine months into the marriage, he decided he couldn't and asked for a divorce. At that point I really thought I was through with relationships with men.

It was at this point I learned about "thoughts are things" and how to manifest what you desire in your life. I began to keep a manifestation journal. In this book I write lists of desires I wish to manifest in my life. I had been through three marriages and divorces, I wasn't ready to take on another permanent, live-in, promise to be with you forever relationship. My children had gone back to Texas to live with their dad. At spirit's suggestion I was homeless at the time and traveling with only the belongings that would fit in my car, but I was lonely. I knew I was totally committed to do hourly whatever my spiritual guidance suggested and I knew a relationship could complicate that commitment. But I also believed God is infinitely creative and could come up with a relationship that would work with my then current lifestyle.

I wrote out a decree stating "I now accept a relationship with a male who is not married, who is available, has no ex-wives or children. He is sexual, sensual, romantic, and adventurous. He must be healthy and willing to be monogamous during the duration of our relationship. He must be willing to travel to be with me once a month for a four day "honeymoon," wherever God has sent me at that time. He must be willing and able emotionally and financially to fly himself or me to that location. He will bring champagne, flowers, milk chocolate, massage oil and a willingness to eat at wonderful restaurants. He will make the plane reservations and reservations at beautiful resorts and hotels. He has his own life and does not need me, but desires to love and cherish me and to be loved and appreciated during the time we have together."

At the time I made this list, it was 1986. I stood on top of a picnic table in Rooster Park, on the Columbia River Gorge and read the decree aloud to the Universe ending with: "I now accept this or something better, through the grace of God and to the highest good of all concerned."

During these years of traveling I did not stay in daily contact with anyone other than my Higher Self. I did, however, send notes to my children and a few friends to let them know approximately where I would be at any given time. One such friend was an ex-lover, who lived in Austin, Texas. I had told him I was on my way to Portland, OR and the number of the family I would be staying with for a few days. I arrived at their home a few hours after making the relationship decree. These people were friends of friends I had met in Oklahoma City. When I arrived they mentioned a man had called and wanted to take me to breakfast the next morning. They gave me his number. I called and found he was the best friend of my ex-lover in Austin and my friend had asked him to entertain me while I was in Oregon. We went to have breakfast the next morning. He was unmarried (in fact had never been married) had no children, was more or less married to his job, which caused him to travel continually. He fit all of the criteria I had listed. We spent time together during my time in Oregon and developed a relationship which led to our traveling and spending time together, just as I had imagined, for several years. It worked well for both of us until my desires changed.

When I once again had a home base, in 1990 I rewrote my decree. I made a list of the attributes I desired in a mate. The list contains 85 items. I've been involved in many male/female relationships in my life so I know what works for me and what doesn't. My experience has been that once we make our list the Universe begins to send "candidates," to see if we will compromise.

When I made my list it did not really occur to me, at that time, the real purpose of relationships. On my list I asked to have someone who was financially independent, hoping to attract someone who would take care of me financially, so I could do my spiritual work and creative work without having to figure out how to care for myself financially. I now know once you make your list it is important to read your list in terms of yourself and to see if you are as developed as what you are seeking in another person. If you are not, you know where you need to begin to work on yourself. If you are married or in a relationship, you do not show your list to that person. If it is to the soul's highest good that person will begin to change to meet the list you have created.

In 1989 I was traveling out of Charlotte, NC and Spirit insisted I was to attend an Inner Dimensional and Inner Species Communication Symposium in Ashland, OR. They also insisted, if I went, I would be a speaker at the symposium. I took my soul's word for it and bought the ticket and flew out. When I arrived sure enough I discovered their female speaker, who was to speak about extra terrestrials, had just called to say she couldn't make it. I explained to the people putting on the symposium who I am and offered my services. They accepted me and allowed me to speak with another presenter who also had experiences with extra terrestrials. This gentleman lived in Mt. Shasta, CA. We developed a relationship and I moved in with him in a beautiful home overlooking Mt. Shasta. It lasted for nine months before spirit was ready for me to move on. Fortunately they didn't require me to marry him. Spirit was very specific about the day I was to leave and the time. I packed up my car and a moving van came. I didn't know where I was going from there when I started packing. During the packing the phone rang and a couple, I had met previously, called to say they had been asked in meditation that morning to offer me a furnished condo they owned in Albuquerque, NM rent free for nine months. I gratefully accepted their offer and moved to Albuquerque. I still continued to travel, but at least I had a home base.

I was living in Albuquerque in 1990 when a woman I had met once called from Oklahoma City and said Spirit was asking her to give me a one woman art show in Oklahoma City. I was amazed, but accepted and we agreed on a date.

I went to Oklahoma City in December for the art show. I stayed with the mother of a man I had met years before at a crystal seminar outside of Reno, Nevada. I didn't know the woman, but she had a large home and was generous enough to let me stay with her. The first night I was scheduled to go to Edmond, a suburb about 30 miles outside Oklahoma City, to speak to a meditation group at a man's home. I met him before when traveling through Oklahoma City. As I was leaving for the meditation group my hostess said she wished I wasn't going out she had hoped we could have dinner and become better acquainted. Usually after talking to a group I hang around and allow people to ask questions so I thought I would be out late, but when she made this comment it came out of my mouth, "I'll be back by 9 o'clock." It was curious to me I would say such a thing. She said, "Well, I wanted to take you to a restaurant where there is a piano bar and they don't usually get started until after nine anyway."

I left and went to the meditation group. The leader had forgotten to tell his people I would be there. There were only two people who attended, so I was in fact able to leave much earlier than I normally would have. My hostess and I went to the restaurant. We ate at the piano bar and watched as people got up to sing with the piano player. A woman got up to sing and when she sat down the man next to her put his arm around her shoulders and gave her a sideways hug. I assumed they were together. After her, the man got up to sing. As he stood up someone from the kitchen called forward and requested he sing Amazing Grace. The request caught my attention. The club we were in was decorated like a bordello. I watched the man sing. He kept his eyes closed. The most amazing gold and green energy sparked in his aura as he sang, which was particularly impressive, since the club was dark. I became very curious to know who he was and if he knew about the energy that came through him when he sang. After he sang the piano player called a break. The man left by a door that led into a hallway and out of the building. I felt disappointed I wouldn't get to meet him.

The woman he was sitting with at the piano bar came over to speak with me during the break. She said, "Well, you have accomplished the impossible." I was confused and asked her what she meant. She said, "You've stolen Charlie's heart and you haven't even said a word yet."

"Who's Charlie," I asked her.

"The man who was singing to you," she responded

"He wasn't singing to me. He had his eyes shut," I countered. "He said he had to keep his eyes closed because every time he looks at you he starts to shake and gets goose bumps and can't think. He's gone to the bathroom and is trying to get up his courage to come and speak to you," she offered. "I want to assure you, he doesn't come here to pick up women. He comes here to sing and usually drinks iced tea. He's a good guy so give him a break." I mentioned the energy I had seen around him and she admitted she was a Reiki healer so knew about energy.

When the man came back he stopped where I was sitting and introduced himself. He was an insurance salesman and a member of a choir at a fundamentalist church. I couldn't imagine how I could have a relationship with a person who was a devout fundamentalist, but one of the things I had written on my most recent manifest a partner list, which included 85 things, was a southern gentleman. When the piano player returned,

Charlie asked me to come and sit with him. I pointed out there were not enough bar stools where he was sitting for me to sit with him. He stated, "I would consider it an honor and a privilege to stand behind you for the rest of the evening." I felt it was something only a southern gentleman would say and so moved to his seat. He attended the art show and took me out to dinner. We spent time together the week I was in Oklahoma City. I enjoyed his company and decided to be very up front with him about who I am and my commitment to spirit. Once I had told him my story and something about my beliefs he said, "I'll never be able to go back to my church now." I questioned what he meant. He said, "Once I heard you speak your truth about the Bible, it makes so much sense to me, there is no way I can go back to the narrow beliefs I've been living my life out of."

During that week I realized he was 82 of the 85 things I had listed. To a practical person this seemed almost too good to be true. I didn't know at that time the Universe sends "looks like" candidates to see if we will compromise our lists. In this case I did. I felt the match of 82 out of the 85 things I had listed was as close as I would ever hope to get to my list. Ignoring the fact he wasn't financially independent and he had no concept of how to manage the small amounts of money he did manage to manifest, I moved to Oklahoma City to be with him. Daily I overlooked the three things he wasn't and enjoyed the 82 things he was. I increased my ability to manifest to include covering his expenses. After three years I began to resent the fact he wasn't living up to his potential and I was working more and more to make up for it. I dissolved our living arrangement.

Later, looking back at the scenario, I realize I had compromised my list because I didn't believe I deserved exactly what I was asking for. I also realized what I did attract spiritually was exactly what I needed in a relationship to cause me to grow in an area where I was still weak, which is the true purpose of relationships.

Since 1993 I have avoided focusing on creating a primary male/female relationship, becoming aware I do not believe it is possible for me to create something I've never seen. In March of 2005 I once again began to think about the possibilities. I confronted God with my beliefs. "I've never seen a male who is all 85 of the things I've written down. I know I can't manifest something I don't believe exists. I can't visualize something that I've never seen. If I've never seen an aardvark I can't manifest an aardvark. How can I manifest something I've never seen?"

As so often happens for me, God's answers come through books that light up or fall off the shelves of my library. The next morning, after my tirade at God, I noticed a book I haven't opened in many years called *The Path of Least Resistance* by Robert Fritz. When I opened the book I opened to a chapter that said: "If you are attempting to manifest something you doubt, fear or don't believe exists – STOP."

"Well, that's not going to get me what I desire," I thought.

"Instead write an affirmation asking to be healed of your doubt, your fear and your disbelief."

"Duhh, how come I never thought of that?"

The next morning during my meditation and study time I wrote an affirmation asking to be healed of my doubt such a male exists, my fear of how having such a relationship would change my life and my disbelief having such a relationship is possible. I suddenly remembered how quickly the Universe had previously answered my requests. So instead of asking for a person who fit all 85 of the criteria for the perfect relationship, I asked the Universe to just send an available male. Someone to date who would enjoy going out to eat with me, going to the movies and maybe traveling or going to the casino with me. I had witnessed couples at the casino together who seemed to be having a fun time. One of my recent spiritual assignments has been to go to the Indian casinos and to set up a Christ Consciousness vortex that will bless the Indians and the people who come to the casinos.

All day, after writing the affirmation, I felt an impulse to go to a certain casino in the evening. I resisted the message. I only go to the casino with a certain kind of entertainment income, disposable income, never income of the organization or income needed to keep all my financial responsibilities current. In that category of income I had $12.00. From Oklahoma City one must drive at least an hour round trip to go to a casino. I was not willing to drive that far with only $12.00. Late in the afternoon I was at my bank cashing the $12.00 check. The inner voice prompted again, "Go to Lucky Star Casino." I finally agreed to drive there, much against my better judgment. After the first thirty minutes I was up $200 and feeling better. I was playing with the "house's" money. I decided to leave my machine to go to the bathroom and to get a drink. As I approached the entrance to the bathrooms a man came out and literally ran into me.

He was an older gentleman and a bit shaky and unstable on his feet. He stepped back but continued to hold onto my shoulders as he looked into my eyes. I recognized him as a man I had dated in 1981, before my spiritual communication started. We were both astonished to be running into each other (literally) after twenty plus years. He was so emotionally moved by the encounter he had tears in his eyes. He held onto me and whispered questions into my ear. He had developed Parkinson's disease, which causes him to whisper and not to be stable when walking. He asked if I were married or in a relationship and if I were now living in Oklahoma City. He was neither married nor in a current relationship. He was thrilled we had reconnected. I immediately realized how I had compromised my list. He was male, available, would love to go out to eat with me, to the movies, to travel, and we were meeting in a casino. I all but slapped myself for my own ignoring of the Law of Manifestation. I knew better.

When I dated him before, I was 40 years old and someone twelve years older than me did not seem old. Now I was 64 someone 12 years older than me, with Parkinson's, seemed really old.

One of my other "beliefs," born of experience with men, is their primary thoughts in relationship to women are sexual. Within the first three minutes of my re-meeting this man, who can barely walk across a room and barely talk, he looked me in the eye and said, "You know I finally got rid of that bed." I could hardly believe it, in his condition it took him less than three minutes to think of me in his bed! I gave him my card and asked him to call me so we could meet in a quieter place to catch up on what had transpired in the past twenty plus years. I knew the meeting had significance and had been arranged by our souls. As soon as I had given him my card and we had parted I felt as if I energetically had a ball and chain around my ankle. I could feel him thinking about me, wondering when we would get together and what it would be like.

In Oklahoma we have a free paper called the *Gazette*. In this paper there is a horoscope written by a man in California who is very intellectual, very amusing and very accurate. The week of April first he prints a funny April fool's horoscope for each sign and then under it he writes the real one. The week after the meeting I read my horoscope. "God noticed you crying in your pillow because he hasn't sent your soul mate. I'm sorry to report God misunderstood and thought you said "cell mate." The real horoscope for that week was, "Write the book you would want to read yourself."

Be careful what you ask for and how you ask. Be sure you are ready. Read your list for your potential partner and see if you are as developed as what you are asking for. The most important thing I've learned in listening and following my soul is to keep my sense of humor. I highly recommend it.

The best affirmation I've ever read for attracting a relationship is from Julia Cameron in her book *Heart Steps*.

"I now accept and draw to me true love...
I draw to myself my right partner,
The soul whose love serves my soul's highest potential,
The soul whom my soul enhances to its highest potential.
I draw this partner to me freely and lovingly
As I am drawn to this partner.
I choose and am chosen out of pure love,
Pure respect and pure liberty.
I attract one who attracts me equally.
I seek and am found.
We are a match made in heaven
To better this Earth."

May you be blessed with relationships that will cause you to grow spiritually through joy, love and adventure.

MANIFESTING AUTOMOBILES

When I left Texas in 1979, to move to Oklahoma City, I had a beautiful yellow, 1977 Buick. The car was paid for. I had manifested it unintentionally by having a serious automobile accident, which rendered me enough money to buy myself and my husband new cars. I had never had the responsibility of taking care of a car so I had no knowledge of how to take care of a car. My husband owned an automotive garage. Within two years of my moving to Oklahoma City in 1979, the car was using more oil than it was gas and was financed for more than it was worth.

In May of 1985 I was asked one morning in meditation by Spirit to sell the greeting card company I had been using as my means of income. I had no idea how to go about selling a company. I thought about running an ad, but before I could even compose an ad a woman called the same afternoon and asked if I had ever considered selling my company. She and her partner brought a check that afternoon and bought the company. I was then asked by Spirit to sell all my belongings, except my car and clothes and a few books and to take my children back to Texas to spend the summer with their father. It was suggested I was going to begin to travel. I was told each day I would be told where to go and the names of the people I was to find. I couldn't imagine traveling in the car I had. Spirit suggested that I buy a new car. They suggested it was blue and had five doors and would get 30 miles to a gallon of gas.

I had just sold the greeting card company and used the money to pay off my credit cards. I had no visible means of income. My car was not in good condition and was financed for more than it was worth. The idea of buying a new car seemed preposterous to my logic. I went to a couple of dealers and each time the salesmen were rude and told me I couldn't afford a new car. That week my son broke out in chicken pox. Needless to say I felt stymied and confused. I yelled at God that if He wanted me to have a new car then He would have to have it delivered to my driveway and I was not going back to any more car lots to be dismissed by anymore males. (Tremendous emotion went out with this request.) That day a letter came in the mail from one of the dealerships I had visited. The dealership had just been purchased by a new owner. The letter was from the new owner. He said he had noticed from their records I had visited his dealership and I had not bought a car. He personally wanted to know why they had not been able to assist me.

I called his personal number and gave him an ear full of how rude his salesman had been to me. I explained after checking the condition of my car and employment he had dropped me off at the used car lot without even introducing me to a used car salesperson. The owner was extremely apologetic. He asked me what kind of vehicle I was looking to purchase. I gave him the description Spirit had given me. The part about five doors was still confusing to me. I had never had a car with a hatchback, so had never considered this as a fifth door. He replied, he had that exact car in his show room and he would personally be glad to show it to me. I explained to him my son had chicken pox and it would be a few days before I could go out again to look at cars and I was now considering another brand. He asked me what kind of payment I thought I could manage. Out of my mouth came, "$200." Since I now had no income I thought I was lying. He thanked me and hung up.

Twenty minutes later the original salesperson who had been so rude to me called. He apologized and said, "I don't know what you said to Mr. Smicklus, but he has instructed me to bring the car and the contract to your house as soon as it is convenient for you." He brought the car and contract. I signed it and he took away my damaged car. The contract included the dealership paying off the bank note I had on the car. I drove this car for three years from one side of the United States to another and back again. The truth was I now needed a van, rather than a hatchback, if I was going to continue to travel.

I wrote out my intention to now accept a blue minivan, with cruise control, cassette player and electric windows, doors and seats. I still had no visible means of income. Shortly after writing my desire and intention I was traveling through Amarillo, Texas and stopped to visit with a woman I had previously met there. I did not mention to her my desire to have a van, but while we were visiting she said, "You know, bj, if you are going to continue to travel I think you need to get a minivan." I laughed and told her I agreed with her but I did not see how, short of a miracle, that could happen. She pointed out her father always bought his cars from this one dealer in Pampa, Texas and she thought if we went to see him that he could help me. Of course she didn't say "father" she said "My Daddy" with a southern drawl. We drove to Pampa and she explained to the dealer I was a friend of her "Daddy" and I needed a minivan. The man did not hesitate; he did not ask about my income, he did not ask how much I owed on the car I was driving. He simply said, "Do you see anything you like?"

I pointed to a blue Ford minivan. He asked if I would like to drive it first. My friend and I drove the car around for a few minutes. All the time we are driving I was in doubt this could happen, because I had no proof of employment and I was still what is known in the car business as "upside down" in my present car. (Meaning I still owed more than the car was worth.) When we got back to the lot the owner took us inside to his office. He asked a few questions about where the car I was driving was financed. He filled out the papers himself and made a call to Ford Motor Credit to assure the financing. I signed the papers and drove away in the van. Trading cars, or buying a new vehicle, has always been one of my least favorite things to do. The van I've been driving now has over 100,000 miles on it and it is time to trade up. The car knows this. A friend just backed into the side of it as she was leaving the driveway. I'm expecting another miracle.

One of our main problems as Humans is our logic. Because of mass consciousness belief our logic will create reasons why miracles can't happen for us. We have a tendency to believe that no matter what we want to do the money has to come first. We are stuck in thinking in terms of money instead of thinking in terms of energy. We came to Earth to prove direct manifestation, to bring Spirit into matter. When we think of a desire, ordinarily our left brain will put a price tag on the desire. We are being asked by our souls to begin to think beyond money. We are being asked to go directly to the desire, to think energetically. Raising our own personal vibration and stating our intentions clearly, with a willingness to accept what we desire through whatever means our soul chooses to use to gift us with our desire, is our challenge.

Our first job is to be clear about what we desire and to be clear energetically from doubt, fear and disbelief. To be clear about what is our true heart's desire. Don't ask for what you want or need; ask for your true heart's desire.

MANIFESTING EMPLOYMENT

The single most important thing about asking for employment is to not see your employment as the source of your supply. Your employment is to be you service to Humanity, the Universe and your soul. For the masses employment equals income. Truly our employment is to be our means of soul growth. It brings us in contact with the people our soul feels would bring us the most growth. We are to choose something we truly love to do in order that our service is truly inspired. Even if you are retired (Spirit prefers we think of retirement as graduation) it is important to have some form of service we perform.

List what you love to do – not thinking about "how will this make me a living." We are not creative enough to think up a job or service to match all of our talents. We are too stuck in the money aspect of employment. There are so many jobs and opportunities out there we've never heard of or thought of. God is infinitely creative.

Several years ago my daughter was in college (she is still working towards her Master's Degree). She was engaged to be married. Suddenly the groom decided he would not be good husband material and backed out of the marriage. Shortly thereafter my daughter found she was pregnant. She was working as a bar tender. The situation seemed overwhelming to both of us. But we sat down and focused on what she really needed, wanted and desired. We wrote about her new job with conditions that seemed would be impossible to fulfill even for God.

She needed a new car. We asked that the new job would pay mileage so that she could get a new car. We asked that the job would pay at least $10.00 per hour. Minimum wage was at something just over $5.00. We knew the job would be part time, so she could continue to go to school, but we also asked for medical benefits for herself and the baby. We asked that she could make her own hours and if it became necessary she could take the baby to work with her. We asked that she could work from home. We asked that she could fulfill this job without having to buy a new wardrobe. Our requests seemed impossible, but we had faith she was doing what her soul intended and she and the baby would be taken care of.

Within a few short days she received a call from a neighbor of the mother of the baby's father. This person stated he did not feel that the father was living up to his responsibility and he wanted to help. He asked her about her intended employment. He knew she had been working as a bartender, because he had hired her to serve as a bartender for some of his backyard parties. He proposed he would call a company that his company distributed for and ask them to create a position he felt she would be perfect for. The position would be one of being a liaison between his company and the company they distributed for. He explained the majority of the work would be for her to drive to each of the fifteen Wal-Mart stores in the Oklahoma City area to straighten the Edy's ice cream. This job did not involve delivering the ice cream only in keeping the display straightened twice a week. My daughter is a Virgo, keeping order is one of her most natural skills. He made the call to his connection within the other company and she did not even have to be interviewed. She had the job. They agreed to pay her $10.00 an hour plus mileage. The stores are open 24 hours a day and she could go anytime they were open and if necessary take the baby in the grocery cart when she went into each store. They gave her a computer, fax and paid for her cell phone.

We, of course, did not know such a job existed; actually it didn't exist until she described it. The Universe created if for her out of our desires. She did not see the job as the source of her supply, she continued to affirm: God is the Source of my Supply. At about this same time I had written in my manifestation book I wanted to be able to offer higher education to my children. My income was minimal and I had no savings. A few days later a man from Phoenix called saying spirit had asked him to provide higher education for my children and he asked what that would involve. He provided tuition and books for my daughter through her bachelor's degree. The medical benefits were provided from other sources and other sources of income came to her. All the needs of the baby were and are fulfilled. The baby's father is a good father. He has the child every other weekend. She is now married to a wonderful man and when she received her Bachelor's Degree the company hired her as a full time employee with all benefits.

Later when her company downsized she was married to a man who could afford to allow her to be a stay at home mom, which had always been her heart's desire.

If we see our employment as the Source, God can only send us what will fit through our paycheck. If we see our work as our "service to the Universe" and continue to see God as the "Source of our Supply" we leave open several billion other directions from which our supply can come.

Understand who you really are and affirm: I AM God operating through my personality for the benefit of Earth all species of life on the Earth and beyond, This will help you to begin to think differently about yourself. And as we think, so shall our life become.

> **We are here to expand spiritual energy in this dimension.**
> **That is why we have come.**
> **That is our purpose.**

MANIFESTING HOMES

In 1987 I had been traveling for a couple of years and was tired and as I would drive myself from one city to another Spirit kept suggesting I write a book. I kept pointing out I couldn't drive the car and write at the same time. I wrote down, if the soul truly wanted me to write. I would need 90 days off from traveling, be allowed to stay in a mountain home, overlooking a creek, with all the utilities available. Within twenty-four hours of writing this request a realtor friend called and said she had a client that needed someone to housesit for them for 90 days. There beautiful log home overlooking Bear Creek outside Evergreen, CO was going into foreclosure in 90 days. They had to leave for Alaska the next day and needed someone they could trust to take care of their empty home. I agreed to stay there. The home was beautiful: 2500 square feet log home, surrounded by 3000 square feet of deck overlooking Bear Creek. The carpets were emerald green. The kitchen and bathroom counter tops were purple. The Jacuzzi was purple. The fireplace was made of Montana turquoise. It looked like the house had been designed just for me. I had difficulty believing I would only be there for 90 days.

On the last day of the 90 days my lover called form Portland, OR and he had just been transferred to Aurora, CO invited me to move in with him. At least I knew where I was going next. This arrangement lasted again for nine months. He was involuntarily retired from his company and began to drink. I had to move on. My friend Judi offered to let me travel out of her basement apartment, which I did for several years.

After I moved to Albuquerque and then back to Oklahoma City I rented a house. My son Cory came back to live with me. After a couple of years the owner wanted to sell the house and I needed to move again. My friend Judi, who is one of the other officers in the Namaste organization, called from Denver to say Spirit awakened her and suggested she refinance her home, take out her equity and buy a home I could use as the Namaste Creativity Retreat Center. I was amazed, but she was sure she wanted to do this.

I went to the post office that day and must have had a happy smile on my face. The young man who waited on me asked why I looked so happy and I told him I was finally going to have my own home. He reached in his shirt pocket and took out a business card. He had just passed his real estate exam.

He came to see me at the rental property at one o'clock that afternoon. I showed him my manifestation book and the things I had written about the house I planned to manifest and the pictures I had accumulated. He said he thought he knew exactly the property I was looking for, but it was currently in disarray being refurbished by the bank that had foreclosed on the property. He didn't want to show me the property until it had been redone. I assured him it wouldn't matter that I would know immediately if it was the right property. I called my daughter and she met us at the address. Just before I stepped onto the porch I looked down and saw a blue feather on the ground. Each time I had become depressed or confused during the years I drove myself traveling spirit would manifest a blue feather to assure me I was in the right place. Kelley and the realtor and I walked up the stairs and half way to the second story my daughter stopped and said, "Mom, the Spirit of the house is saying 'rescue me, rescue me.'" Her affirmation gave me even more chill bumps.

Judi came to Oklahoma and placed a bid on the house. She was able to buy the 3500 square foot home for $140,000. Compared to the prices she was usually dealing with in property in Denver it seemed an amazing bargain.

In my manifestation writing I had asked that the property have a view of a large body of water. The first property spirit had shown me when I was looking on my own was across the street from the city water tower. Spirit was trying to teach me to be more specific in my description of my desires. Before we had looked at this property with the realtor I had changed the writing to say a view of a lake or river. The property he took us to has a view of a river from the back yard. The back yard had never been developed and had thirty years of packed dirt. My manifestation book showed decks, a koi pond, flowerbeds, a sunroom and lots of bird feeders. Within a few months of moving in I checked on the price of having the sunroom built. Before I called for quotes I asked my soul what the sunroom would cost and the figure I was given was $15,000. The first salesman came and measured and figured and gave me a bid of $26,900. I said, "Well, then you can't be the right contractor, because God said it was going to cost $15,000."

"The young man looked stunned and said, "What did you say?"

I repeated myself and he said, "Just a minute," and began to scribble on his clip board. He came back with, "Could you live with $15,900?"

"I think I could," I responded, "but how can you change the price so drastically?"

He laughed and said, "Well, if God said it should cost $15,000 I'd better get as close to that figure as I can."

I borrowed money from some friends who have lots of money and had the sunroom, decks, koi pond and flowerbeds built. Within a few months of living in the home all of the other things from my manifestation journal were in place.

A few years later the upper story of the house needed to be painted. I did not care for the color the bank had chosen, but had tolerated it with the intention that when it needed to be painted I would have the upper story covered with vinyl siding. Neither Judi nor I had the money to pay for the siding and having it installed. I cut out a picture of a house similar in design to mine with siding and put it by my phone and energized the picture each time I answered the phone.

I had heard about a discussion between Deepak Chopra and Maharishi (the founder and leader of the Transcendental Meditation group) back before Deepak wrote his books on manifestation. Maharishi mentioned he intended to build meditation temples around the World and Deepak asked him, "Maharishi, where is the money going to come from to build them?"

Maharishi responded, "From where ever it is now."

After hearing about this conversation I began to hold that thought. The money we needed for the siding or the siding itself was being moved energetically from where-ever it was now to where I needed it to be.

At this time, I was asked by my soul, to go to all of the Indian casinos nearby to Oklahoma City, to create vortexes of energy in each one to bless all who entered there. Each time I went to one specific casino I saw the same man no matter what day or what time of day I went there. I watched him closely because he always seemed to win. I never spoke to him and he never spoke to me. A few days later a group of men came and began to install vinyl siding on my next door neighbor's house. I was furious. I raged at God what part of my address did you not understand? A couple of hours later, after I had calmed down, I went next door and asked the workmen if they would send their boss over to give me a bid on what it would cost to have them put siding on my house. When their boss arrived at my door he was the man from the casino. I was shocked, but knew for sure I had the right contractor to do the job, but I still didn't know how I would pay for it. Judi happened to be in town and they agreed on the price and he agreed to come and do the job the day after we called and told him we had the money.

A couple of days later I received a call from a friend who lives in Minnesota. She called saying spirit had suggested she call because whatever was going on with me she needed to be a part of it. I explained about my desire to have the siding put on the house and about the man from the casino. She said she would speak to her husband about the idea of loaning me the money. She never called back so I decided her husband probably would not agree to the loan. We were all meeting shortly thereafter in Sedona for one of the Namaste Gatherings and she and her husband were attending. When they arrived she took me to the side and apologized for not getting back with me. I said I understood and that I had assumed her husband didn't want to make the loan. She explained he was uncomfortable loaning the money to Judi, since he didn't know Judi. Again, I assured her I understood and not to worry, the money was on its way from where ever it was now. She said, "But he would be willing to buy the house from Judi and in the mortgage transfer we will take out enough money to put the siding on and to pay off the loan you made to build the sunroom. Then you will only be responsible for paying rent to keep the mortgage up to date and we will be responsible for the maintenance and give you life estate to the property." This was the "this or something better I had asked for from Spirit."

4.

Principles Of Truth

In the Human consciousness, there are many basic principles. I call them the Principles of Truth. Honor is one, trust; integrity, respect, and acceptance of others are some of the main ones. There are more, but if we are expressing true honor in our daily living the others seem to fall into place naturally.

We each come into life with a certain unrecognized mission. We forget the contract we signed with our soul before we reincarnated. Our basic mission is simple, but we make it complicated. The mission is first and foremost to make ourselves more of what we really are and less of what we are not. Because there are so many errors in the mass consciousness beliefs, and we take these on instead of truth, we don't remember we are a spirit seeking to have a Human experience. Mass consciousness believes we are Humans trying to overcome sin to become spiritual. We buy into the consensus reality. Consensus reality means the vast majority of people see life in a way that is generally agreed as being the way it is. If we are going to make ourselves more of what we really are and less of what we are not, we have to get clear about what we really are, which is a Spirit having a Human experience.

We are each conscious Beings. This consciousness, which is who we are, is an energy frequency. In that frequency is a record of all our previous lives in great detail. Some people call this the Akashic record; some people call it cellular memory. When we learn to communicate with our souls we can have access to our own Akashic record. If it is part of our mission to read for others and we have integrity we can eventually have permission to access the Akashic record of other people.

What we focus on in our daily lives is what we get. Most people think they understand this, but few really do. For example, if you have a problem and focus on solving the problem, come up with a solution and then apply it, most people would then expect they have finished with the problem. If you focus on the problem, looking for resolution, your focus is the problem. So you solve the problem, but the focus remains, the focus is problem. Not a problem, or the problem, but simply the problem. We are problem focusers. We create problems so we can solve them and feel smart. The problem is not a problem, or the problem, but simply problem. If problem is the focus, then problem remains, and the whole problem cycle will begin, or rerun, all over again. Because we believe we need problems, we believe in problems and we believe in problem solving.

In any governing body and in most people's lives, the focus is on how to solve problems: the war on drugs, the war on hunger, the war on terrorism, how to stop smoking, drinking, doing drugs, over eating, lack of this or that. We get more of what we think about. What we focus on expands. What is it you most think about and talk about? How many people do you know who constantly talk about their health problems, their money problems, their relationship problems, their work problems? The result of our attempt to solve our problems is anxiety. First of all we claim ownership of them by calling them "my problems."

To any thinking person it would be obvious there is a purpose for the life of Humanity. Although I don't meet many people who take time to have much original thought or what I think of as investigative thought, most thought is repetitive and borrowed based on borrowed beliefs. We are designed to be reasoning, creative Beings. There are Universal Laws that govern this creativity. Our learning experience involves living and experiencing what we create. There is no time off from creating. Our creative ability doesn't shut down as long as we are thinking. Our thoughts and words are the focus for our creation. In other words, what we think about is what we create. The vast majority of people think and talk about what they least desire in their lives. People think more about what they do not want in their lives than they do about what they desire.

Every thought we have is creative. Creative thoughts eventually manifest into a physical expression. That physical expression is our life because we create our own reality. In the past it has not been common knowledge that we are doing this, it is still rare to find people who understand this. Most people are still in complete denial that what they think has anything to do with what they experience and would mock anyone who tried to convince them they create their lives by what they focus on, what they think about. But, whether they mock it or accept it, it continues.

If we are experiencing something in our lives that we do not want, continuing to focus on not wanting it reinforces our continuing to have it in our lives. Focusing on the problem, focusing on what we don't like about ourselves or our current reality doesn't change it, it continually reinforces and maintains the current reality. The only way to change it is to think something else, focus on something else. We must focus on what we desire instead of what we see there now.

Truth reveals itself to us when the time is right. Timing is everything. At one time in our lives we can hear a Truth Principle and pass it off as nonsense or dismiss it or miss it completely. But when the time is right and we hear a Truth it hits us, shocks us and sometimes brings us to tears or laughter. Truth is life meeting you in the moment and revealing itself to you. When you're ready you hear it, notice it and if you're really ready you act on it. It is easy to hear it, understand it and still go back to our old habits of thought and action, back to our comfort zone.

When a Truth hits your heart it begins to percolate. The heart knows the Truth, but to the brain it is a stranger. The brain will attempt to convince us of a different reality, the consensus accepted reality. The heart knows. The heart is the seat of the soul.

If you are reading or hearing this information you have brought yourself to a very creative place and time in your life. Your soul desires you pay respectful attention to this opportunity to know the Truth. Sometimes we finally hear the Truth when we've given up or when we feel desperate. Desperation opens doors in our mind; complacency keeps these same doors closed. It normally takes something dramatic to break a person's attachment to their comfort zone, but sometimes it is just soul timing. When the time is right the information reaches us through whatever means the soul chooses: a book, a person, a lecture, a movie, a chance encounter.

Our lives—as we know and experience them—are made out of time: second by second, minute by minute, hour by hour, day by day, week by week, and so on. This is the substance of your life. Everything we perceive ourselves to be is formulated and made from habits and conditioning of time.

If in the formation of your character you are always late for appointments, for meetings with people you care about and respect, meetings with people you love, for special events in your life, you sow into your life the seed idea you're not worthy of either their respect or of any respect for yourself. As you continue to regularly be late—because it doesn't matter to you— that weed seed germinates and grows, flourishing in the decay of your self-respect and the loss of respect of the people around you. A pattern is established, a habit that from such unrecognized beginnings, can be very destructive in your life. Being late is a subconscious, rather than a deliberately conscious way, of letting other people know where your life is and where your priorities are. We choose to be late at such a sub-conscious level we don't consciously realize the messages we are sending to others about our lack of respect for ourselves and for them and their time. Always being late shows we are not ready to take control of our lives.

Truth is life meeting us in the moment, revealing itself, but we are seldom aware in the moment. We are usually focused on the future or the past and what is happening in the moment often slips past us unnoticed. We think at a rate of several hundred words a minute never realizing our thinking creates our life. We need to choose carefully what we think, because what we choose to think creates our life. If you do not like your life as it is, the first step is simple, change what you're thinking. Most of our thinking has been what I call trash talk or trash thinking. Most of it is self-judgment or judgment of others. Thoughts create your focus and focus creates your life's reality. So, change your thinking about what you do not like about yourself and find something you do like about yourself to focus on. If the people in your life are people who focus on what's wrong with life you need to get away from these people. One of the most difficult things about changing ourselves to be more positive is the people we've hung out with will feel uncomfortable with us and we will feel increasingly more uncomfortable being around them and listening to them complain, blame and not take responsibility for their thoughts and what's happening in their lives. You cannot make new changes if you are overwhelmed by old programs. And if your friends are living the old programs, then they are not truly your friends; they are your handicap. Changes in ourselves often require we get new friends and leave old friends behind. People who are addicted to suffering think they are normal. They believe life is about suffering or is to be suffered.

The addictive nature of Humanity has accepted lives and life- styles far below their potential, both below their material and spiritual potential, because it is easier. Apathy dominates most of our society. Thinking stagnant sameness is normal or their "lot in life" is a common Human belief.

If we are making an effort to give up drinking, we don't hang out with our old gang at the bar. If we are making an effort to eat a more balanced diet we don't hang out with our friends at the all you can eat buffet. For many people, a life of hostility and emptiness is normal. They blame the government, their parents, the police, the system, anyone but themselves for the state of their lives. Many people find it easier to accept this as normal than to continually frustrate themselves with thinking there is something more. The truth is there is something more, but change requires courage. The courage to want something more and the courage to think differently is required for positive change. You cannot change and remain the same. You cannot change and hang out with people who are unwilling to change. We want to change, but we also want to keep things as they are in our lives and this can't happen. If you think change is going to be hard, it will be. If you think and believe life is hard and difficult, it will be. If you focus on and believe it can be and will be easy to bring positive and uplifting change into your life, then that is the reality you will create.

When you use a word repetitiously you empower it, because it comes from you, it is you who receives the benefit of its creation. Life is shitty, life is hard, life is difficult, my life is confusing, I am tired, I am sick and tired of this, this situation is impossible, are all examples. These sayings are all repetitive words creating repetitive reality.

When a catalyst enters our lives, we are thrown into making choices. Our sub-conscious program wants us to stay the same, reinforces sameness. Our soul wants us to change. Change has the power of newness and dynamic energy. We are always in a struggle between sameness and change; both are always present in the Human psyche. We often shut down to the idea of changing by using drugs, alcohol or just the excuse it would inconvenience or scare someone in our lives like our friends, our boss, our partner, our children or the people in our church. We are under great pressure from the people in our lives to continue being the same individuals we always have been. We are pressured to conform. We are expected to remain as we were. Do not fight the pressure, nor resist. What other people think and expect of you has nothing to do with you, nor can you control it.

Change is not easy. We didn't get where and how we are overnight. It took a lot of time and effort. Effort is required to bring about change. There is no quick fix, but what you are attempting to achieve is balance. Balance is a response to life rather than a reaction. Reaction is fear-based, a repetitive conditioning from the past. Love responds while fear reacts. Our inner buttons are constantly being pushed daily in our normal lives. Every time you make the choice to stop and respond to a challenging situation or person in your life, rather than to automatically react, you are leaving old habits and conditioning behind. Which of these two ways of living—reaction or response—do you think is going to offer you the most creative and supportive lifestyle?

We become the thoughts we think and speak aloud and we become our attitudes. People who are very sensitive often over eat to build a wall around them as a false protection system to try to shield their sensitivity. Some people eat to become larger, because they feel small; they feel insignificant or without power.

If you can't love the body you're with, love the body you're in.
Face your natural physique and feel good about it.

We have a need for affection from the people we love, but if we develop a dependency on others for our self-worth, reassurance of our worth, or dependency for a sense of security we will always feel insecure. The only true security comes from our direct knowingness of our soul. If we came into this life with a constant need to be reassured we will have chosen parents and eventually spouses who withheld what we needed so we could learn to give it to ourselves. If we came in to heal our inner emotional imbalance, we will choose people who make us face it, by not giving us what we think we need from them. At some point we must decide to like ourselves, to love ourselves and not to expect to get validation and love from outside ourselves. Your well-being can be nurtured and supported by others, but it can never be developed, given or maintained from anywhere other than within yourself. You are not inadequate.

We might decide on the desire to be the slim and fit person we once were. I desire to be quick, sure and capable. I desire to look in the mirror and like what I see. I desire to be fully emotionally capable within myself. I desire to lose my dependency on others for emotional support. I desire to like, love and approve of myself and accept myself and stop blaming myself for everything that goes wrong. I desire to be a person I can be proud of and respect. I desire to know I lack nothing intellectually and my social status and financial income in no way reflect an inadequate intellect.

We are required to live what we desire, not simply to desire it. Wanting never has, nor ever will, supply what we desire. It all has to do with focus. Energy flows where we focus. Our lives are made up and fabricated from the substance of what it is we focus upon. If we focus on self-pity, emotional dependency, sexual frustration, lack of friends, lack of funds, lack of health, lack of positive attention from others, then we attract and maintain exactly what it is we want least in our lives. Our minds do not know the difference between what we do want and what we do not want; it will attract. Left to themselves our thoughts will naturally gravitate toward our problems. We have to rethink everything. Self-pity attracts more reasons into our lives for us to pity ourselves. Criticism is one of the most powerful and destructive forces we can unleash against ourselves. How much of your thinking is self-critical? Everything you criticize in yourself by your focus you develop, maintain and enforce. Nothing positive will ever come from self-criticism.

When we self-attack we have no possibility of self-defense

Fear is our greatest enemy. We fear what other people think, we fear loss of health, loss of love, loss of friends, loss of money, not having money, fear disapproval, losing our jobs, fear of IRS, fear of being attacked, fear of losing our homes, fear of losing our spouse or family or means of financial support, fear of growing old and becoming helpless, fear of loss of memory, etc. If we cannot see the source of our own fear, then there is no room for change. Fear will always cancel out change. The main pastime of sameness is to create more fear, because fear will defend and maintain sameness. Eventually the risk of staying the same has to become greater than the fear of change. What other people think of you has absolutely no effect on your life unless you take their opinions and create an effect. It is what you think that affects your life. Life is not about words from the intellect, it is about action based on intelligence.

You have to be open to change, or at the very least it helps. Change is going to happen whether we are ready or not. Change is the only constant in life. We can make choices and control change or let it happen by default. Change is a catalyst in life that is ever present. Change may enter your life at any moment and blow it apart. Generally, people resist change. They prefer more of the same, even while hating it. Our resistance to change generally can be measured by the degree of our daily suffering—and there are many levels and forms of suffering. The more we resist the constant push of change, the more we suffer. Openness and a willingness to go along with change no matter what it demands, is rare. The more you oppose your thoughts the more they will oppose you. Wrong focus literally creates and feeds opposing energy.

Life is not a physical reality.
Life is a spiritual reality of which we have a physical experience

Our awareness and focus determine our experience of reality. Whether we live in a limited consensus reality, or a limitless greater reality, is entirely up to us. Neither is right or wrong, or good or bad. It is all about choosing. Although you have a physical body, and that body is yours, it is not who you are. You are a magnificent, metaphysical Being of Light. This is your Truth. And, if you focus on and live this Truth, then Truth shall set you free. If you believe nothing beyond a linear reality, then you will live half a life.

Truth shared with proper timing is Truth received. With out proper timing, they are simply words that add up to something that the intellect thinks it knows. The intellect knows the sum meaning of the words, but it has no idea of the wisdom they contain. Wisdom is not the meaning of words; it is connecting with the essence of the contained experience. Wisdom is not a linear experience, it is a spherical experience. In other words, what you perceive as wisdom is held in a simultaneous moment that brings the past and the future into the now. Wisdom is a heart event, not a head event. Heart experience is special, while head experience is linear. The heart is about intelligence while the head is about intellect. Truth must be lived to become empowered and actualized. Truth, as words of knowledge only, is conceptual, empty and powerless. You must live Truth to know Truth. Truth is an experience. Do not fight anything in life, not even sickness; embrace it, learn from it, then release it. Nothing comes into our lives by accident.

As long as we look to blame, we empower and maintain blame. By taking responsibility for ourselves and our lives in each moment, we move out of, and beyond, the negative bonds of the past. We can change jobs, move to another area, change relationships, but we take ourselves, our conditioning, our attitudes and our beliefs with us. Until we change, it doesn't matter where we go, there we are.

Once you have established a good honoring relationship with yourself, you will find life rewards you. If you honor yourself, you honor life, and if you honor life, life will honor you. There is nothing more honoring in your life than to take responsibility for yourself and your life. Think of yourself as worthy and deserving—and life delivers. Think of yourself as unworthy and undeserving—and life withholds. Be aware of what you think. The deeply programmed, sub-conscious thoughts are the ones that run your life. They are the thoughts you are not aware of thinking until you begin to pay close attention. Listen to your thoughts without criticizing them. Create deliberate thoughts of self- appreciation, self-acceptance and self-respect. Knowing your own capabilities is part of wise living. Wisdom is the art of knowing your limits, but not allowing them to limit you.

Humanity went to sleep en mass.
Waking up is a one-by-one experience

We are unlimited spiritual Beings. We are only limited by our thinking. True success is to live our potential. Unlike other creatures on the planet, Human beings have the ability to transform themselves.

Become a scriptwriter of newness instead of writing
more of the same

5.

HowTo Be Authentic In A World That Demands Conformity

From birth, we are born to be like our parents genetically and culturally. We are taught to believe as they believe, to act as they act, to sound as they sound. We are born into this World that operates with certain systems, most of which demand conformity to certain rules or beliefs. In order to survive we conform to these rules and beliefs. For many of us there comes a time when we begin to question these rules and beliefs and desire to find out for ourselves if these things we have been taught are really the REAL truth. This usually causes struggles within our families and relationships.

In my case I was born and raised by a mother, who was weak-willed and weak physically. I grew up with a message and belief that women were weak. Only at mid life, through surviving a series of very difficult circumstances, did I find this belief is false. I am a strong woman. What a difference it would have made in my life had I grown up believing I am a strong woman, that women are strong?

Many people were raised to believe in a God who is to be feared and obeyed. What a difference it would have made in our World had we known God is loving and desires to assist us in all things.

Too many people suffer from self-sacrifice, self-abuse, self- loathing, self-deception, self-pity, self-serving and self- immobilization. What are the cultural beliefs you've grown up with that you would like to now change about yourself? You can. You can change yourself to be the person you really were meant to be rather than the one your parents, spouses and society have programmed you to be. Pray daily for the courage to learn how to transform self-loathing into self-loving through passionate choices.

The first step in becoming authentic is to question, "What do I believe?" What do I believe not only about God and the World, but also about myself? What do I believe I am capable of achieving? Why do I believe I'm not capable? When we ask these sorts of questions and seriously seek answers we will usually uncover a time in our lives when someone told us we were not beautiful or attractive, not capable, not smart enough, too slow, too weak, too poor to be what we dreamed of being. These things were and are lies. They were told to us by fearful people who needed to control us in order to make them feel better about themselves. They were people who needed to control us, because if they didn't they knew we would become greater than anything they had ever allowed themselves to become. Often they told us these things in order to keep us from becoming disappointed by temporary failures. Do not allow convention to hold you captive.

If we look at and challenge these beliefs we usually find we have toned ourselves down, diluted ourselves, been less than we know we are capable of, in order to try to fit in, or be acceptable to someone else, to gain someone else's approval, acceptance or protection.

NO ONE CAN GIVE YOU YOUR SELF-WORTH, BUT PLENTY OF PEOPLE CAN ROB YOU OF IT

The truth is we are God acting through these personalities. Remind yourself daily, "I am God acting through my personality for the benefit of Earth all species of life on the Earth and beyond." This is the truth about you. Once you can start operating from this premise and begin to give up other people's beliefs about you, you can become authentic.

The underlying sense of sadness most people feel, that yet unnamed feeling, is a result of not being in touch with our authentic selves. We may accomplish much of what we set out to do, but somehow something still seems to be missing, we still feel that sense of there must be something more. At the end of life more people regret what they didn't do, didn't try than regret what they did do. Ask yourself, "If I died tonight what would I regret that I didn't do?" If I live another day is there a choice I can make that will enhance the quality of my life? Find the courage to do what you have to do to be happy in this life. "The only courage that matters is the kind that gets you from one moment to the next." Mignon McLaughlin.

WE ARE THE CHOICES WE HAVE MADE

Authenticity pushes us past our comfort zones. We often settle for being less than we are because of fears. What do we fear? Success? Failure? Survival? Death? We can choose to be ruled by our fears or we can face them and excel. If we have a fear, such as a fear of speaking in public, we can arrange our lives so we don't have to speak in public or we can find ways to begin to speak to small groups of people about topics that interest us and our audience and develop the muscle of being able to overcome the fear and speak in front of a group of people, knowing that God is speaking through us. If we have a fear of flying we can make an agreement with a friend to take a flight and sit on the aisle seat and pretend we are sitting on a bus. Or call forth Angels to keep the plane in the air. We can develop a faith in God and our souls that says we understand we will not die until it is time for us to be through with this life. Death is an illusion. The only thing that dies is the body. We continue to exist.

You don't get to choose how you are going to die or when.
But you do get to choose how you're going to live

Joy is the absence of fear. When we choose to give up our fears through confronting them and finding they are illusions we will experience more joy. We will begin to understand the Laws of the Universe. We will understand if a relationship does not work out, if we do not get the job promotion, or the house or the car, it is because it is not to our highest good to have this at this time. We will begin to respect and understand divine timing. Being grateful is the first step in feeling more joy in our lives. Gratitude is the first step in having abundance.

For most of us there were things we loved once, but have chosen to live without. Can you think back to the best moments of your life? I challenge you to begin to remember what those things were for you by sorting through magazines and tearing our pictures of things that appeal to you. Make a collage of these pictures to remind yourself of what makes you happy what brings you joy. These may be things that made you happy in the past such as books, films, clothes, furnishings, pets, playthings, vacations, holidays, food, flowers, hobbies, gardens, TV programs, comforts, comic strips, fantasies, music and magazines or places you liked to hang out, like the library. They may be things you remember from childhood. I challenge you to begin to reinvest them in your life. You will discover your authentic needs (your soul needs) and your passionate yearnings.

We will remember as children and young adults who our heroes were.

Who did we attempt to emulate? What qualities do these people have, or seem to have? In many cases they were actors, also playing parts in movies and we were admiring who they were pretending to be more than we were admiring who they really were off screen. We too can decide to play a part, but this part will be authentic. It will be based on our own personal truth and our own personal choices.

Look at the way you dress, is this the real you, or someone else's opinion of how you should look? When you shop do you purchase what you really want, what really excites you or do you buy what's on sale or what will make you look like other people? Do you buy what's in style or do you buy what you know looks good on you?

Once we decide to become authentic our souls will begin to co-create with us soul-directed events. Events that will challenge us to be who we were designed to be rather than the robotic person, the fearful person we have been.

Our authentic self knows the truth. When we allow it to have voice in our choices rather than overriding it with the societal beliefs it will guide us to make choices, which will cause us to feel joy, spontaneity and love. Our lives will change. They will change through crisis, chance or choice. The lives we are living now are a result of the choices we have made thus far. We are often fearful of making choices because we do not trust our instincts. Unconscious choices are how we end up living other people's lives. You can't make a wrong choice. You can make a choice that will cause you to live an alternative future. There are many possible futures for each of us. When you look back you can also remember intuitively you knew which choices were not to your highest good, but you chose to ignore your intuition, therefore you got to live out the lessons. Our individual choices dictate which futures we choose to live out. If we look back, we can see that often when we made, what we thought was a bad choice, we learned many things we would otherwise not have learned.

What if you were told today that in one year you could be living the life of your dreams, what would it look and feel like? That life can be yours as a result of the choices you make every minute of every day. Every choice we make takes us closer to or farther away from the life we desire. This includes every thought we choose to think about the World and ourselves. It makes all the difference to believe you live in a benevolent Universe, the child of a benevolent God than to believe you live in a hostile Universe with a judgmental God as ruler and judge of your every action.

Life isn't about survival. When we live survival lives we are opening ourselves to have experiences that will teach us lessons through pain. When we choose to live lives of choice based on preferences we will live lives of extraordinary coincidence. Even when we are living lives of choice we will have periods of seeming dormancy. These are gifts from the soul. Take the periods when seemingly nothing is happening and use this time to reflect and to plan.

By being your authentic self and having authentic success no one can take it away from you by their actions. If someone chooses to fire you or divorce you, you still have yourself, because you are very aware you are not your job, you are not your relationship. You simply begin to make other choices of how to share your authentic self in another circumstance.

THE NET ONLY APPEARS WHEN WE ARE IN MID AIR

Passion is the basis of authenticity. Passion is not just about sex. To live an authentic life is to live your life with passion and compassion. Spirit defines compassion as the ability to combine our passion with that of another to feel their truth and to be willing to share with them. In our lives we will often come to a point of choice between desire and duty. We must always be willing to live with the consequences of our decisions.

THERE IS A CLUE AT THE HEART OF OUR FRUSTRATION

It is always important, not just to look at how much we have, but also to look at what we have escaped. Just by choosing to be born in America we have escaped restriction and persecution. All our acts have sacramental possibilities. It is important to celebrate everyday epiphanies.

God grant me the serenity to accept
The people I cannot change,
The courage to change the one I can
And the wisdom to know it is I.

EVERY RELATIONSHIP WE HAVE IS A REFLECTION
OF THE RELATIONSHIP WE HAVE WITH OURSELVES

This chapter is inspired by the reading of "SOMETHING MORE" Excavating Your Authentic Self by Sarah Ban Breathnach author of *SIMPLE ABUNDANCE* two of the best books I've ever read.

6.

How To Create Your Version Of Heaven On Earth

Above the entrance to all of the ancient wisdom temples were the words:

KNOW THYSELF

Because you are the only one you will never leave nor lose, you are the one you have the most responsibility to get to know most intimately. You are the only answer to the questions of your life. You are the only solution to the problems you have created

in your life. It is essential you like yourself, feel you are worthy of respect, admiration and love. It is vital you believe yourself deserving of all good things. In order to do these things, you may have to let go of who you thought you were and what you have assumed your life was about.

We do not experience the World as it is.
We experience the World as we are.
Excavate and co-create

We create our reality by our perceptions based on the thoughts, feelings, beliefs and expectations we have of ourselves, others, the World and God. In the beginning, it is important to examine and challenge each belief we hold, each perception we have to see if it is truly ours or is a programmed perception that came from our parents, friends, teachers, church officials or the media. If we keep our current views, beliefs, limitations, fears and misperceptions, which are all fueled by the media, we stop ourselves from becoming all we were created to become. To develop our own truth requires introspection, sorting and beginning to reject what we determine is not true about ourselves, the World, the Universe and God.

In my family, we were taught self-love equaled being selfish. We were not taught to love ourselves and certainly not to know ourselves. To know ourselves would have required introspection and it was continually stated, "Too much thinking can make you crazy." I grew up to be a master of patching up whatever didn't look good to the outside World. I had a master's degree in "making do" with what was available, which was usually very little. I was proficient at keeping personal matters out of sight and of causing things to look as if they were always running smoothly. Staying in control became a full time job. I accomplished this at severe expense to my health and my own personal desires and feelings, but to the outside World it always looked good.

When I tried to explain how I was feeling to others they told me, "Get over it. You've got everything. What you have should be enough for anyone. Don't make trouble for yourself by wanting something that doesn't exist. Be happy with what you have." They tried to convince me I did not have a problem, so I began to feel I was the problem. I thought, "Something must be wrong with me if I can't be happy with this life." I had become a reflection of what I did and had.

When the seismic shift began to happen, cracks began to appear and the truth began to seep through the illusion I had been living as my life. When I began to explore my inner life, which is where the books assured me my truth lies, all I found was a garbage heap in the form of fears, shame, anxieties, angers, grief, sadness and regrets. I was plagued by the fear I was not enough and a deep sense of lack, although I wasn't clear about what I lacked. When I looked inside, I was appalled by the number of self-deprecating opinions and insecurities I'd been holding inside and keeping at bay by staying overly busy and pretending my feelings didn't matter, because they were uncomfortable to me and made others angry or uneasy when they were expressed. I learned what might make others angry and I hid those feelings inside.

When I finally located a mentor who did not think I was crazy, he said, "Stop making yourself wrong about your thoughts and feelings. Instead, consider your discontent, worry and fear are really personal truths challenging your current reality. In order to change, you must first recognize you are stuck and agree to do what it takes to become unstuck." The very thought was frightening. I somehow knew if I changed, it would cause repercussions in all the people around me.

I found the search to find out who you really are requires a willingness to look closely at what you are not, the false beliefs, the things hidden in the dark place inside you. What is required is we observe what is there and decide if we want to keep it. Is this the truth and does it serve me now? If it no longer serves you, allow it to float away in a balloon of knowing. Always replace it within yourself with an affirmation that is your new truth, your new perception about yourself, the World, God.

I found, when my mind would fall asleep on the job of being willing to look inwardly, my body could be counted on to wake me up, I could feel the "feather" of my intuition and be brave and follow it, or I could ignore it and wait for the two-by-four experience that would make clear the truth I was ignoring.

Some two-by-four experiences are auto accidents, loss of a job, lack of purpose, depression, loss of a loved one, addictions, rape, a near death experience, insomnia, divorce, bankruptcy, illness, loss of home space, an unplanned pregnancy, personal injury, having your home broken in to, having your car stolen, finding out your spouse or partner has been unfaithful, losing your purse or wallet. Life's two-by-fours are great awakeners, but initially they can be so painful we only want the sleep of depression. We may be too stunned by the pain, fear, resentment, anger or upset to see the value or lesson of the experience. It takes courage and time to go beyond trauma. What is important is waking up to answer the recurring knock of the feather or the two by four, because then we can transform our lives and, thereby, transform the World.

Once I was brave enough to overcome the belief I should ignore my feelings, I found what happens inside me is what makes my life work. If I ignore what I'm feeling and thinking my life will not work in my favor.

The greatest obstacle to our attaining anything we desire in life is our "comfort zone." Our comfort zone is our familiar way of functioning automatically or without consciously thinking about what we are doing. The same thoughts, followed by the same actions reap the same results. To do the same things day after day in our lives and expect a different result is a form of ignorance, ignorance of the Law of Cause and Effect. While living in our comfort zones, we often resist change, even positive change, because it is unfamiliar. We spend a lot of time and energy protecting and defending the constricted, stress-ridden reality we call our life, our everyday thinking. This is the energy we could rechannel into creating the life we desire.

Change is constant and inevitable. The Universe is not static; it does not remain the same. Our bodies are in a constant state of change. The deep ruts we have created in the ways we think and the habits of our everyday activities need to be looked at. Are the results of these thoughts and these behaviors bringing me the life I desire? If not, why not? Complaining gets us more of what we are complaining about. Worry gets us more of what we don't want, because it gives permission for universal energy to go to literally what we are worrying about rather than to what we desire. It wastes our energy and time. To change our lives we must first agree to think differently and to act differently. We must set new intentions of thought and behavior.

Since change is inevitable, the primary purpose of setting goals and intentions is to allow ourselves, to a greater degree, control over the changes in our lives, change by choice, rather than being served "potluck" as a result of allowing others to make our choices for us.

Early on in my life, I was hesitant to set goals for fear I would not be able to accomplish them. I thought, "If I never write them down I will never have to feel like a failure if I don't accomplish them." I later learned if I don't write down my heart's desires my soul has no permission to assist me to accomplish them, because of the Law of Freewill. I learned our purpose is to be co-creators with our souls, to co-create our individual version of heaven on Earth, and, thereby, to ultimately recreate heaven on Earth globally. It can only be accomplished one life at a time. If the word "goals" is a buzzword for you, as it was for me, you may need another word. I now use intention or affirmation.

I write the intentions in present tense. I affirm "I AM" as often as possible. "I AM" is a reference to our higher Self, our God Self, rather than our ego self. Without roles, what remains is the "I AM" part of us. This is the part of us that exists before, after and between births. The ego creates the roles. In order not to be in internal conflict, our goals must be in harmony with our basic values, our souls, our purpose for coming to Earth for this particular incarnation. The I AM, the spark of divinity inside each of us, wants to show us the truth about ourselves, our talents and the peace and magnificence we are capable of manifesting.

I don't recommend you ask yourself, "What do I want or need?" Take a deep breath into your heart and ask yourself, "What is my true heart's desire?" Close your eyes and let an image or answer come. If nothing seems to occur to you, take more breaths into your heart and keep repeating the question with each breath. When the answer finally comes "from your heart" rather than from your mind; tears may accompany it, because our true heart's desires are also our soul's desires. We have usually devalued our true heart's desires by claiming we can't have them, so why try to want what you can't have. We tell ourselves things like, I don't have the money, education, time, or talent. I'm too old, too young, too fat, too ill, too committed to my children, to my job, spouse, or parents, etc. God is infinitely creative. These excuses are illusions we have created for ourselves to stop ourselves from disappointment and possible rejection.

Try this exercise daily until you begin to receive responses from your heart, your soul. Then write your desires in present tense as if you are already experiencing that life. We need to set goals or intentions in all areas of our lives in order to remain balanced. These might include:

Health goals
Personal goals
Family goals
Career/work goals
Financial goals
Spiritual or inner development goals
World goals

Our intentions or goals need to be challenging, but believable in order to not be overwhelming. Make sure one goal or intention does not contradict another.

People who do not have personal goals are doomed to work for those who do

It is important to write and read our intentions in present tense, because they describe our desired results of our intended life. If we state them in the present tense, we are more likely to work to do the next single thing toward accomplishing them now rather than holding them in future context.

I now accept...
I AM now experiencing... I AM now enjoying...
I AM now grateful for...

Example: I AM now accepting a life filled with joy, adventure, love, beauty, friends, fun and health, with money and time in excess of my needs and desires.

Read your affirmations daily with enthusiasm and emotion. You are sending these messages into your sub-conscious mind to replace the erroneous messages you've held there, with your new truth. You are sending these "purchase orders" into the Universe to be acted out to the highest good of all concerned in alignment with the Divine Plan of the Creator.

You may want to write them on 3x5 cards and carry them with you to read anytime you have to wait or to keep a set in the drawer of your desk at work or write them on your computer. You may choose to make a poster of words and pictures that place these desires into your sub-conscious visually. You can also do this in a notebook form. I do all of the above and it has changed my life. We can argue all that would take too much time, but I can assure you it is time well spent. Writing it out, in as much detail as possible, gives your soul a blueprint of what you desire. It also gives them permission to help you to achieve it. It keeps you focused on action rather than living your life passively, sitting back waiting for the next two by four.

In my case, when I breathed and got in touch with my true heart's desire, I had to let go of who I thought I was and what I assumed my life was about. I had to give up the familiar for the unknown. In the beginning my goal setting was vague. At that time, I could not even begin to imagine the life I have co-created now. I had to begin with what I could believe. Life is a process. Goal setting is a process and can be an ever-changing process. Sometimes, after living with an intention for a while, I find it isn't truly what I desire and I change or replace it. Setting intentions gives our lives direction, without which we have a tendency to wander around unfocused or to stay in familiar ruts.

For our lives to become different, we have to first be able to imagine or pretend (pre-intend) ourselves in different circumstances performing different roles intentionally from our "I AM", our God Selves, our hearts. It is important to remember we are always playing roles. The trick is to write your own script, choose your own costumes and choose the other characters with whom you desire to share this stage of your life. Allow the "I AM" Self to play the role through you by staying in touch with that I AM part of you, by staying deliberately connected to your soul through your heart.

7.

Intution

Inside, we have the I AM, our ever-present consciousness that will urge us to become who we really are. It will prompt us to be more loving toward ourselves and others. This is the voice of our intuition.

Always hold an intention to seek the highest truth that can be revealed to you at this time. The ego is invested in preserving the status quo. It will put up a fuss when challenged with new information.

Living from the outside in does not bring the peace of lasting happiness. Living from the inside out may at first be confusing and may seem difficult, but it is the way to inner peace, freedom from fear and lasting happiness.

Life as we know it is often interrupted. It is important to stay totally present where we are and to stay conscious of our feelings and all that is happening around us. Trust and ask:

WHAT IS THE NEXT SINGLE THING FOR ME TO DO OR KNOW FOR ME TO BE IN A STATE OF DIVINE GRACE?

This question, which was given to me by my soul, gives the soul permission to give us the next intuition that will lead us in the direction of potential connections and events our souls have set in motion. The next step to take us toward our goal will be revealed or present itself. It may, however, not appear to have anything to do with how we "think" a person would move toward their goal. In my experience, God's methods seldom match my logic. I have discovered through the years of following this method and it leading me to my own personal form of heaven, God doesn't move us in a straight line.

Getting connected consciously to my soul was like digging deeply within myself and after making my way through the garbage heap of my erroneous beliefs I found a ball of golden thread. Holding the end of this thread keeps me connected to my soul consciousness. As I follow where the golden thread leads the ball unwinds and I become aware of more of my true self. God seems most interested in leading us along a path that is about meeting people and developing loving relationships.

During the five years I traveled constantly, I often felt I was being sent in circles or spending a great deal of unnecessary time retracing paths I had already followed. But, when I would go back and spend time with people I had met on a previous visit, they would introduce me to people they had met since I had been there before or people who had been out of town when I was there previously. Sometimes on my return visit to an area, people would be visiting from another country and meeting these foreigners, as they visited the United States, often saved me from having to travel abroad. Eventually, I did have to travel abroad to fulfill my mission.

In my case, Spirit was using me to connect a network of people who would eventually be invited to gather occasionally to meet each other and to develop further relationships between these people from various parts of the World. Often we will only see in retrospect why our intuition led us to a certain place and sometimes it will seem as if no connection was made, nothing happened. The reason being, occasionally the other person we were to meet did not follow their intuition to be at that location at the same time we were asked to be there. In those cases, depending on the meetings' importance to the souls, another potential arrangement for meeting will be arranged.

Cosmic timing is important to our souls. To us, it may seem cosmic timing takes far longer than we would prefer. If we ask our souls lots of questions about when a certain thing will happen, very often their reply will be "soon." To us, "soon" would mean in terms of days or hours. Since the soul operates a non-time related vibration, the word means nothing, but is a way of keeping us moving in the direction of our goals with hope it will come to fruition soon.

I learned after many frustrating years not to ask when or how, but to only ask for the next single thing for me to do or know to be in a state of divine grace as I move in the direction of my goals.

The gift of Freewill, given to Humans by their Creator, is our greatest gift. God trusts us to be brave and to make the right choices, the choices suggested by our souls. The information given to us by our souls is always a suggestion and never an order. We always have the Freewill to ignore the intuition, the suggestions of our souls. If we ignore the suggestions, the soul must allow us the freedom to make choices that will lead us into difficult or challenging situations.

When I first started receiving information, from my soul, I did not understand this concept. I thought I <u>had</u> to try to do everything that was being suggested no matter how difficult or unprepared I felt and no matter the financial cost to me. After years of following the soul's suggestions to travel homelessly for years, I had accumulated $26,000 in credit card debt most of it at 21% interest. I was ready to quit following the suggestions of my soul and to settle down and get a "real" job, a job where I received a paycheck. When I explained I was quitting working for the soul and following their advice, they explained their suggestions had been just that, suggestions, not demands or dictates as I had taken them. They stated that I had always had my Freewill and could have refused or negotiated conditions under which I would agree to attempt the task being suggested. They said our association was always meant to be a co-creation, but that I was allowed to assume as much responsibility as I chose, without expecting their help. I was angry and appalled the soul had not let me know this sooner in our relationship.

"I'm not traveling anymore until I'm out of debt," I stated.

"Fine. This is how to get you out of debt," was the soul's reply. "List all of your debt. The left column is the total debt itemized by individual or company to which the monies are owed. The right hand column is the monthly responsibility you have to that debt. You will have two totals. At the bottom write a statement that releases this energetic indebtedness to the Universe. State your desire and intention to live in a state of solvency and being continually debt free. Money is energy. It represents an exchange of your time and energy for what you desire to have or experience. Agree to continue to gratefully pay monthly toward the debts. Write the checks with the same enthusiasm you would write thank you notes. You are actually thanking the Creditor for trusting you with what you have already purchased and are using. Checks for electricity, health care, transportation, clothing, food, cable service, insurance, water, fuel, or a roof over your head should be viewed as slips of gratitude."

I followed the directions even though I had no belief it would work, but within a year I was living debt free. The money came in the form of an unexpected inheritance, from a friend I had assisted and not as a result of the hours I was working doing readings and classes. I was following guidance to do the next single thing and the soul was arranging to move money, energy, from where it was now to where I needed it to be to balance my indebtedness.

SUMMARY

1. Find your own truth by listening to your thoughts. Change your thinking and you change your life.
2. Write down your true heart's desires in present tense in as much detail as possible.
3. Release these desires to your soul and the Universe to be acted on to the highest good of all concerned in alignment with the Divine Plan.
4. Ask your soul continually, "What is the next single thing for me to do or know for me to be in a state of divine grace?"
5. Expect an answer.
6. Have the chutzpah to follow your intuition, even if you are not sure, move in that direction.
7. Live as if the true definition of you is: "I AM God operating through my personality for the benefit of Earth all species of life on the Earth and beyond", because this is the truth of who we are.

See form for getting out of debt on next page:

To get a clear image of your financial condition, list your current financial indebtedness or responsibilities.

	Total Balance	Monthly Responsibility
Mortgage or Rent		
Car Payments		
Utilities:		
Gas		
Electric		
Home Phone/Internet		
Cable TV		
Cell Phone		
Water/ Sewer		
Subscriptions		
Bottled Water		
Maintenance		
Car Loans		
Bank Loans		
Credit Cards		
Capital One		
Chase		
Master Card		
VISA		
American Express		
Discover		
Department Store		
Personal Loans		
Insurance		
Personal		
Medical		
Life		
Auto		
Renters		
Mortgage		
Taxes		
State		
Federal		
Other		

Totals:

I now release this indebtedness into the Universe. I now accept its immediate and complete payment through rich avenues of Divine Substance. I now accept being totally debt free through financial abundance. And so it is!

8.

The Universal Law Of Attraction

HOW TO GAIN DELIBERATE CONTROL OF YOUR LIFE
UNDERSTANDING THE UNIVERSAL LAW OF ATTRACTION

That which is vibrationally like unto itself is magnetized to itself.
You get what you think about whether you want it or not.

There are Universal Laws that affect everything in the Universe, the physical and the non-physical. These Laws are in effect and working whether we believe in them, understand them, or not. They are eternal and operating everywhere simultaneously. We can deliberately use this Law and create what we desire, or we can ignore it and create by default. Once you understand all people, circumstances and events are invited into your experience by you, through your thought, you can begin to change your life by changing your thoughts. Trust me, when I first heard this information I thought it to be so much BS. I did not believe what was happening to me was in any way connected to how I thought or the beliefs I held.

Being told I invited unwanted things into my experience through my attention to them sounded ridiculous. How could I possibly be in control of what was happening to me? I didn't have control of all these other people who were causing me to

feel afraid, inadequate and undesirable. This had to be their fault. I was totally committed to being concerned about what other people thought and expected of me. I had been well taught by my mother that to worry meant you cared about the person you were worrying about.

One of the first books I read in my progression was Terry Cole-

Whitaker's *What You Think Of Me Is None Of My Business*. I was horrified I allowed <u>what I thought other people thought of me</u> to control so much of my behavior. It took me quite a while to figure out they weren't usually thinking about me at all. Most of the expectations I placed upon myself came from what I projected they might be thinking or might be expecting. Then there was Napoleon Hill's *Think And Grow Rich*. I read it several times and still wasn't convinced what I thought was going to make any difference in what happened in my life. Then I came across Florence Scovel Shinn's *The Game Of Life*. The language bothered me, and all the *Bible* references bothered me, but the simplicity and energy of what she had to say stuck with me. Her examples were outdated, but I decided to try writing down a few of my desires, just in case what she was saying was real. As soon as I began to write down my desires, and to use a few affirmations, things began to change. I didn't stick with it, because actually it frightened me to see what I was writing and what I was thinking actually began to happen. The idea I could be that powerful was scary.

A little later, after I had made a direct connection to my soul, I came in contact with Sarah Ban Breathnach's *Simple Abundance*. This book changed my life. I got serious about creating a more beautiful, simple, abundant life. My soul explained that one of my missions in coming to Earth was to demonstrate manifestation and to teach manifestation. Sarah's book encouraged me to start a gratitude journal for writing down what I was grateful for on a daily basis. Her affirmations were in simple language that I could relate to. I began to make a manifestation book and posters with cut out pictures of things I desired to attract into my life. More positive things began to happen. This time I didn't feel as much fear. If this was my mission, I figured I'd better keep going, even if it scared me. I gave up being homeless and created a home, I attracted a loving relationship. I got out of debt. I began to accept I AM an artist, writer and teacher.

I learned <u>not</u> to use words like want and need, since my subconscious mind and my soul were always listening to my thoughts and taking me literally. I understood to use these words made my soul and sub-conscious mind think I wanted to stay in a state of wanting and needing, rather than having and accepting. I learned to listen to what I was thinking. Monitoring my thoughts, I caught myself limiting what could happen by what had happened in the past. I had to learn to overcome believing if something was going to happen it was completely up to me to <u>make</u> it happen.

In the first message I received from my soul, I was told my job would be to state, in writing, my "true heart's desires." In the beginning, I didn't know what I desired. I had only ever thought in terms of what do I need to survive. It was suggested I breathe into my heart and ask myself over and over, "What is my true heart's desire?" I did this until the truth began to surface. I had so successfully hidden my desires behind belief in limitation, undeservedness, doubt, fear and disbelief it took a while for me to admit the truth to myself and to my soul. I would suggest now if you don't know what you desire, or if you think you don't desire anything more than what you already have, you might begin to ask to have your desires revealed to you by your soul. When you do this, the soul will begin to put ideas in your mind or bring you in contact with things that interest or intrigue you.

We didn't come to Earth to survive; we came to thrive. It does not serve the World for us to play at being small. We are miraculous creations of God. Our purpose is to allow the soul, that created us, to operate through us. Our job is to remember we are not the body. We are the Spirit that inhabits the body. The soul created the body for its use in this dimension. Ask to know your purpose, the purpose for which the soul created the body. Ask for what is yours by divine right and under grace, in a perfect way.

Things are attracted to us by our emotions, thoughts, vibrations and actions. We have a responsibility to keep our vibrations as high as possible. What will come to us will match our vibration. Be sure to raise the vibrations of your food, drink, supplements and medications higher than the vibration of your body by putting your hands around it and mentally stating the request, "I now raise the vibration of this higher than the vibration of my body." Hanging out with people who choose to remain stagnant, choose to think and expect negativity, and do not serve us or our souls lowers our vibrations. We have a responsibility to avoid exposing ourselves to the negativity of the media. This does not mean we have our head in the sand. It means if something happening in the World is our responsibility to know, our soul will make sure the information reaches us. The newscasters and weather reporters are interested in drama, ratings and creating excitement. We have a responsibility to be at peace, to focus on peace, beauty, harmony and love. We create what we think about. We receive the essence of what we think about.

We have a responsibility to create our own World, to let others choose their own World. This is what it means to be in the World, but not of the World. We cannot send out thoughts of peace and love while exposing ourselves to images of disaster and mayhem.

It is extremely important for us to pay close attention to our emotions. Our emotions are an indicator of whether we are focusing on things we desire or things we don't desire. They are signals from the soul as to whether we are moving toward or away from our goals.

How you see yourself and how you define yourself is important. The truth of who we are is, "I AM God operating through my personality for the benefit of Earth, all species of life on the Earth and beyond. This is the truth of who I AM." When we think of ourselves in any other way we are limiting the truth and not allowing the soul access to the body and our thoughts. To define ourselves by our job title, our relationships, our nationality, our religious affiliation or any role we play is an error. We are not our roles and we are not our bodies. We are Spirits here to have the Human experience. We are not Humans attempting to become spiritual. We are spirits attempting to be Human.

When we worry, we are misusing our creative ability. We are working to manifest what we don't desire. We get what we fear and what we worry about. It takes the same amount of energy and focus to think about what you desire instead of worrying about what might happen. When we think about what we lack, we create more lack. When we think about disease or the possibility of having an accident, we invite that into our lives. The more you think about illness, talk about illness, and worry about illness, fear illness, the more you attract illness. I desire to remain healthy and to have strength and vitality. When you think of someone as a pain in your neck or a pain in your ass, you can give yourself a pain in that area of your body. When we are stiff- necked, stubborn about not being willing to change or to see another person's view, we can also create a stiff neck for ourselves physically. When we are afraid to move forward in our lives, we will usually create problems in our hips or knees. When we are afraid to reach for what we desire, it usually shows up in our hands, wrists and shoulders. When we don't stand up for ourselves, often the legs will begin to fail us. Being around someone who irritates us usually causes us to have a sinus problems. Holding onto irritation about anything will cause an irritation in our bodies. There is usually a sub-conscious reason we would choose to be ill or disabled in some way. I have several friends who have decided they don't want to challenge themselves to work for a living so they have created disabilities severe enough to qualify for Social Security disability.

Some of the affirmations about health that I use:

- I desire, intend, claim, accept and am now grateful to receive perfect health for myself and my family.
- My body is free of all diseases, fungi, pain, viruses and misqualified cells.

- The miraculous healing Cosmic Power is now flowing through me and permeating every atom and cell of my body.
- Every cell and organ of my body is now complete and perfect and functions according to Divine Law.
- God is hearing and seeing through me; my eyesight and hearing are perfect now.
- My heart is strong and works perfectly to carry blood and oxygen to every cell of my body.
- My body is radiant, healthy, beautiful and strong.
- My hair is thick and easy to manage and my nails are strong.
- I give thanks for the continuous healing that is taking place in my body, mind, Spirit and memory.
- My teeth and gums are strong and healthy now.
- My body releases toxins and waste materials daily, easily and painlessly.
- My skin is soft, firm and retains its elasticity.
- The energy of God, in and through me, forever cleanses, heals and renews every organ and every atom in my body after the pattern of perfection.
- My heart is a living center through which the Love of God flows to bless me and all others I encounter. I AM a birth less, ageless, deathless Spirit.
- I intend joyous survival, joyous creating, and harmony.
- I intend to eat well and to be comfortable in my body.
- I AM surrounded by people with whom I AM harmonious.
- I AM erasing every pattern of disease in my cells, my sub-conscious mind and restoring the pattern of perfect health.
- I manifest my I AM Presence through this body now.
- I AM Spirit; perfect, holy, harmonious. I manifest my true authentic self through this body constantly.
- God in me is infinite wisdom; I always know just what to do.

The Cosmic Healing Power, which made my body and all its organs, knows all the processes and functions of my body and the miraculous Healing Power is permeating every atom of my being, making me whole and perfect. All my organs are God's ideas and, through the power of the Almighty God, they are all functioning perfectly now.

Spirit, Divine Life and energy flow freely to every part of my being, cleansing, revitalizing and restoring me to Perfect Health.

I now surrender every personal doubt, fear, or hard feeling that might retard the perfect flow of life through me. There is no obstruction in my mind, my veins, or my affairs. I AM harmonious, peaceful, free and courageous.

The Laws of Harmony, Grace, Beauty and Balance are governing my life now.

I AM filled with peace, strength, power and decision of Spirit. I AM complete and perfect now. My body is pure spiritual substance and as such it is perfect and harmonious.

It is important the affirmations you choose to use are in words you would use, Express what you desire your sub-conscious to believe.

Our sub-conscious and our souls do not understand humor. When we say things as a jest, the subconscious takes us literally. When someone asks you how you feel and you respond, "I feel like I've been run over by a Mack truck," we are inviting just that sort of experience. One I hear people using now a lot is, "He threw me under the bus." Don't assume because some television program says it is cold and flu season you need to accept you will get the flu or will automatically get a cold. You get what you expect. You get what you focus upon. You get what you affirm. Be very careful what you say after the expression "I AM." Make an effort not to use such terms as, "Give me a break" or "that breaks my heart."

Every thought we think has creative potential. Every thought we think while feeling strong emotion is even more likely to happen quickly. We have a tendency to affirm something positive and immediately discount the thought by thinking it isn't possible if we can't figure out how it would happen. The "how" is God's job, our soul's job. Being clear about what we desire and writing it down is our job. It is important to replace in our vocabulary the words desire and accept for the words want and need.

When you are feeling down, make an effort to think a thought that is a bit more uplifting than what you are currently feeling and move to that vibrationally. Usually it helps to think of something for which you can feel grateful. It is difficult to move directly from depression to joy, but you can move gradually from depression to feeling a bit more optimistic, a bit more grateful. Then to move from that thought up to something a bit more hopeful and on and on until you get yourself up off the couch and once again functioning. Don't attempt to go emotionally from zero to sixty in one moment. It won't work.

When you are feeling disappointment it is a clear indication what you are focusing on is not truly what you desire to experience and is usually an indication you have put someone else in control of your happiness or your future. Usually when I feel disappointed I can look back and see I did not project clearly the outcome I truly desired to experience.

The Universe, your subconscious and your soul do not distinguish between what you see and what you imagine. This is why our imagination is one of our greatest gifts. If we can imagine it, the World and the Universe will work with us to create it. Whether the imagining is positive or negative is not censored by the Universe or your soul. This is why what we really desire, we get, and why what we really don't want, we also get. This is why it is important to make what you truly desire to be your most dominant thought and vibration. Thought and emotion are the stuff that is the vehicle through which all things are attracted or created. Guide your thoughts in the direction of things that feel better and better.

To desire a wonderful life is not selfish. We desire for others what we also desire for ourselves. We can only assist those in other countries, who are suffering, by visualizing them fed, clothed, housed and well. The positive energy we send with these visions can cause miracles of change to happen in their lives. Imagine them in a better situation, successful and happy. The greatest gift you can give another is the gift of your expectation of their success.

When you find yourself in the midst of a painful situation, or with a seeming insurmountable problem, ask your soul for a solution, not an answer or a fix. An answer then has to be figured out by your mind, a fix will surely need to be fixed again, but a solution is a method to dissolve the situation. Turn your undivided attention to the successful resolution of the situation, not focusing on the situation as it appears.

Allowing others their right to be how they are is one of our most difficult challenges. Especially when we think we know what would help them or solve their situation. We are here to be examples of demonstration of good in our lives. People will not come and ask us how to suffer. They have that figured out, but if our lives look like fun, healthy, interesting, successful lives; people will ask us how we did it. Then we can share what we know of the Law of Attraction. People only learn by example.

When you write out your desires, I have found it to be helpful to use the phrase: I desire, deserve, intend and now gratefully accept_____
_____. This phrase includes all the components of manifestation; desire, intention, belief, expectation or anticipation, present tense and gratitude. At the bottom of each page of desire descriptions I always write: "I now accept this or something better through the grace of God

and to the highest good of all concerned." I have learned the soul is always thinking bigger than I seem to be able to imagine and this clause gives them permission to give me something even better than I have been able to imagine.

Humans have a tendency to only believe what they have seen or previously experienced. The mass consciousness belief is that to become wealthy one must win the lottery, marry rich, inherit wealth or work really hard. Once I got the example, God had created 6000 varieties of just begonias, it occurred to me She was probably capable of thinking of more than four ways to solve any problem I could create. Sometimes you can envision how a thing can happen, but more often than not when we try to do this we are getting in the way or limiting how it could happen. Visioning is good, but only if we vision the end result not the method of how to get there. Leave the how to the soul or the Universe; focus only on the desired end result and ask continually, "What is the next single thing for me to do or know for me to be in a state of divine grace?" After you ask the question, be prepared to do what you feel intuitively is your next step. My experience is, it is not useful for me to try to figure out how the next step I intuit which is mine to do has to do with me getting the end result I desire. In my experience of working with the soul and God, I'm pretty sure the straight line method of being the fastest way to reach a goal has not occurred to the soul. They are always more interested in the people I will meet along the way than in efficiency or expediency.

I have recently learned the power of action in the direction of my desire. When we moved into the Center, I had large, long, tiered flower beds built all across the back yard. I must have thought I would be 40 forever when I did such an expanse of flower beds. Keeping weeds and grass out of them became a real issue. I noticed that I enjoyed container gardening much more than planting in the flower beds themselves. I began to envision having them cleared out and filled with landscaping fabric and mulch and then putting containers of flowers on top of the mulch. My action in that direction was to purchase the supplies. A few days later, a couple of the ladies in the Thursday night class asked me what I intended to do with all the supplies I had piled on the deck. I explained my vision and they said they would love to help, which they did, and it now looks exactly like my vision.

My grandson gave me two bird feeders last year which he painted lavender, my favorite color. I have many other bird feeders in the yard which were not attractive. Last week I decided to buy paint and paint them all lavender. I went to the store to get a can of paint and a brush, rather than cans of spray paint, because in Oklahoma we have very few windless days. I waited in the department for someone to come to mix the paint for me and no one came. I walked around and discovered six cans of lavender spray paint on sale. No other color was on sale. I took it as a sign I would be able to spray them and bought the cans. The next morning I woke up, to one of the few still days in Oklahoma and sprayed them all, and they look lovely.

When I was still homeless I was in a fabric store one day and saw a design of violets and I asked the store clerk for a swatch of the fabric for my manifestation book. Years later, when I got to have the Center to live in, Waverly, the maker of the fabric, had sold that particular pattern to Target and everything I could imagine desiring, sheets, curtains, comforter, wallpaper border, pillows, ceramics for the bath, shower curtain, dishes were all available for me to have. I've never tired of the pattern.

Years ago I met a woman in Ben Lomond, CA, who had a benefactor who provided a place for her to run a retreat center. The person gave her life estate to the property, which meant she could live there as long as she desired or as long as she lived. I wrote that down as one of my desires. Years later I was living in a rental property and the owner decided she wanted to sell the property. I began to look for another place to live. One of the things I had written down was I desired a view of a large body of water. The first house my soul directed me to look at had a view of the city water tower across the street. I had to laugh and go back and rewrite the desire to "view of a river, lake or creek". Soon after, a friend in Denver called and said she had been asked, by her soul, to refinance her home and to take out her equity to purchase a home for me to live in and to use for the Namaste Creativity Retreat Center. It is important to remember other people are also listening to their souls and some are brave enough to follow their soul's suggestions even when it means taking risks. My friend bought the house we now live in and use for the retreat center.

The things the house didn't have that were on my list: a sun room, decks and koi pond were created during the first year. I borrowed money to build the sunroom from friends in Denver and paid on it monthly. Before I called the builders, to get a bid on building the sunroom, I asked my soul what it would cost and the reply was, "About $15,000." So when the salesperson came and gave me a bid of $26,900, I told him he was the wrong person to do the job. He asked, "What do you mean?" I explained that God had said the job should cost $15,000. He said, "Just a minute." He began to write again on his clipboard and in a few minutes asked, "Could you live with

$15,800?" I agreed, it was close and asked him how he could come down so much on his price and he stated, "If God said I should charge around $15,000, I guess I'd better get with the program."

I never liked the color the bank had painted the wooden upper story of the house. When it needed to be repainted a few years later, I asked the owner if we could afford to have the upper story covered in vinyl siding. Neither she nor I had the money to accomplish my desire. She attempted to refinance the house, to take out money to get the siding, but nothing seemed to work. At this time, one of my jobs for the soul was to go to all of the Indian casinos in Oklahoma to set up vortexes of positive energy in each one to bless the people who worked there and the people who came to gamble. I placed a picture of what the house would look like with the siding beside my telephone and every time I answered the phone I energized the picture of my desire.

Every time I went to a certain casino, I would see the same man no matter what day I went or what time of day I went. I never spoke to the man, but watched him intently because he always won. A few days later a crew of men started putting what I considered to be my siding, on my next door neighbor's house. I was angry and asked God, "What part of my address did you not get?" After stewing for a while, I went over and asked a workman if he would ask his boss to come over to give me a bid on what it would cost for them to put siding on my house. When their boss showed up at my front door it was the man from the casino. You can imagine my surprise. I tried to convince him if he started the job the money would come. He stated he believed in God, but he just wasn't that trusting about money. He did agree to do the job the day after I had the money, which was a concession on his part.

Years ago I heard of a conversation Deepak Chopra had with Maharishi, the leader of the TM movement. Maharishi told Deepak it was his intention to build meditation temples all over the World. This was years before Deepak wrote his books on manifestation. Deepak asked Maharishi, "Where is the money going to come from to do this?" Maharishi replied, "From wherever it is now." I decided to look at my situation from that viewpoint and began to affirm the money is on its way from wherever it is now. A few days later a friend called from Minneapolis and asked, "What's going on with you? Spirit says I'm supposed to be a part of whatever is going on with you." I explained about the siding, the man from the casino and about our being unsuccessful in restructuring the current loan. She indicated she might be able to lend us the money for the siding. After a few weeks I had not heard back from her and assumed her husband had been unwilling to make the loan. We were all meeting in Sedona for the next Namaste Gathering and she and her husband joined us. She took me to the side and apologized for not calling me back. I told her I understood and not to worry, the money was on its way from wherever it was to where I needed it to be. She said her husband was reluctant to loan the money to Judi since he didn't know Judi. He would be willing to buy the house from Judi and restructure the mortgage to pay for the siding as well as paying off the loan for the sunroom. They had also decided to give me life estate to the property and to be responsible for all the maintenance.

When I left Oklahoma City to travel in 1985, my soul asked me to sell all my belongings except what would fit in my car, which I did. They assured me in the future when I needed furniture, etc., again it would be provided. In 1991, when I moved back to Oklahoma City, the friend who had loaned me her furnished condo in New Mexico offered me the furniture contents of the condo, stating she had two other homes and didn't want to have a garage sale.

During the years I was traveling, I had very little income. My children came of the age it was time for them to go to college. I wrote in my manifestation journal, "I now accept being able to offer my children higher education." A few days later a man called from Arizona and said during his meditation Sprit had suggested that he offer my children higher education and wanted to know what that would involve. Only one of my children took him up on his offer and gained her degree. Again, I offer the idea to you that other people are listening and are sometimes brave enough to follow their guidance.

A few years ago I wrote, I now accept receiving $30,000 to be able to take off a year to write and finish some of the books I had been working on. I attended a workshop in Minnesota. A man was there whose family is wealthy and his job is to disburse money from the family foundation. After the conference we were walking down the hall and he said to me, "I think I've made a mistake. I think I've contributed to the wrong Namaste." The

next morning at breakfast the director of another Namaste organization tossed a check from his foundation for $30,000 in front of me. My immediate thought was he had corrected his mistake and the check was mine. The other person did not know of the error and demanded I read for her to tell her how her soul wanted her to use the money. You can imagine this was one of the most difficult lessons of my life.

GOD IS THE SOURCE OF MY SUPPLY

There is a continuous movement toward me of the supply of money and all I need and desire to express my fullest life, happiness and action. I desire, intend and now gratefully accept I AM a prosperous person whose wallet is always filled with cash and my mailboxes are always filled with negotiable checks made payable to me or to Namaste of Oklahoma. I AM always able and willing to pay all of my financial obligations before they are due. I AM totally debt free through financial abundance.

We can never have enough money to make us feel secure. Money can be stolen, burned, devalued and destroyed. Never make your feelings of security dependent on the amount of money you have. Develop financial serenity and what you have will feel like enough.

- I now accept total financial freedom and abundance. My good is assured me by God, the Indwelling Essence of my life.
- I AM free to be myself and free to follow Spirit's suggestions. I agree to express that which is ready to express through me now from my soul.
- I stand in the midst of eternal opportunity, which is forever presenting me with evidence of its full expression.
- I AM peace, joy, happiness and contentment. I AM the Spirit of Joy within me. I AM the Spirit of Peace within me, of poise and power.
- There is One Life and that One Life is expressing consciously through me now. I now release any blockages or beliefs I have had to allowing total financial abundance.
- I see my bank account and my wallet continually filled with all sufficiency to meet every need with surplus to share.
- I AM totally debt free through financial abundance.

It is important to remember to ask and to ask in writing. We are in the middle of the Fourth dimension. The Laws of the Fourth dimension are different than the Laws of the Third dimension. In the Fourth dimension, in order to allow our souls to assist us, our desires must be in writing.

SOONER OR LATER WE REAP THE FRUITS OF OUR THOUGHTS

We are responsible not only for holding visions of our personal desires, but also for the desires for the Earth and all of Humanity. We came to make a difference. We came to demonstrate the Law of Attraction in a positive manner. We came to co-create our version of Heaven on Earth. Please take the time to think about it and ask your soul to show you your true heart's desires. Give up any, "Yes, but," mentality. Give up things like, "but I don't have the money", "I'm too old to start over", "Yes, but I don't know how to paint, write, tap dance, whatever". If it can work for me, it can work for you.

If you are in debt, be brave and list your debt, face it and work toward reducing it, but also release it to be paid through rich avenues of divine substance. Asking to be totally debt free through financial abundance eliminates the possibility of having to claim bankruptcy. When I did this the first time, I was $26,000 in debt in credit cards, most of which were at 21% interest. Within a year, I was debt free through one cash donation of $1,000 and through a person who left me a $25,000 CD at the time of their death.

You don't have to believe it works to begin to try it. I didn't and now I wouldn't live any other way.

OUR MIND CREATES OUR REALITY

Spirit feels we need a better understanding of the natural Laws of the Universe and how to apply them in our own lives. We live in a spiritual Universe. God is in through and around us and for us. No one has seen Cause, Universal Mind or God, but we have seen results that effect of Original Cause is life. The only proof we have of mind is that we think.

Thinking should not be an automatic thing; it should be controlled. Our body is not self-operating, it can be changed by thought. Decide to consciously think and decide. Give up habitual thinking. Unconscious, habitual thoughts are the cause of misery in the Human condition.

Memory is a result of conscious thought. Memory is an unconscious operation of what was once a conscious thought. What a realization when we realize by changing our thought we can re-mold our bodies and our lives; right thinking can improve our life and body.

No one has ever seen the great Cause which lies behind all manifestation of life. We only see the physical evidence. That is our proof that God exists.

God exists in everything. God exists in us and because God exists in us, we are able to recognize other beings in which God exists. Spirit is the medium through which we are conscious of ourselves and others and our environment. Our thoughts are operative just as radio messages are operative through Universal Medium. We are being consciously or subconsciously affected by the thoughts of those around us.

The Universal Medium of Mind is one of the attributes of God; the avenue through which God operates as Law. One of the most difficult problems we have is to realize when we are dealing with the Law of Mind, we are dealing with an absolutely impersonal thing. It knows how to create, without knowing what It creates. We must distinguish between the Law of Mind and Spirit which uses the Law. Spirit is the Power that knows Itself. There is Infinite Law, which knows how to create, but does not care what It creates.

There is a Law in the Universe which operates in a certain way according to the tendency set in motion; it does so mathematically. We cannot destroy this Law, but we can learn to re-direct Its movements. It is like the soil in that it does not know if it is making a turnip or a tomato, the consciousness is in the seed. We can plant seeds and later decide we desire something else, we go out and uproot the first seeds and plant others in their place. We are not changing the soil we are simply using it in a different way. The Law is the doer of the Word, the Word is our thoughts.

God as Law means the way in which Spirit works, and Law in this sense is the servant of Spirit. Our bodies are a manifestation of Spirit. The Trinity is the Thing, the Way it Works and What it Does. The Thing is Absolute Intelligence, the Way It works is Absolute Law; and What It Does, is the result–manifestation.

The definition of Spirit is: "Life or intelligence that is not physical. It is vital essence, force, energy, distinct from matter." The nature of being is unity, with three distinct attributes: Spirit, Soul, and Body.

Spirit is the active and Self-conscious Principle. Spirit is first Cause or God, the Absolute Essence of all that is. It is the Great Universal I AM. Spirit is Conscious Mind and is the Power which knows Itself. It is Conscious Being. It knows nothing outside Itself. It is the Principle of Unity behind all things. The masculine and feminine principles both come from the One Spirit and are all Life, Truth, Love, Being, Cause and Effect. It is the only power in the Universe that knows Itself.

It is impossible for a finite mind to comprehend such a complete Life and Power. In moments of inspiration we realize to a degree that God is All, the Life in Everything and is the Creative Force within everything.

The Soul of the Universe is the receptive medium into which the Spirit breathes forth the forms of Its thought. It is subjective to the Spirit. That which is subjective is always impersonal, neutral, plastic, passive and receptive. Creation doesn't mean making something out of nothing

Creation is the passing of Spirit into form and is eternally happening. The only active Principle is Spirit, Self-conscious, Self-Knowing Life, and all else is subject to its will.

The great teaching, of great thinkers of all time is we live in a three-fold Universe of Spirit, Soul, and Body, of Intelligence, Substance, and Form. The Law is the servant of the Spirit, and is set in motion through Its Word. Law does not know Itself; Law knows only to do. It is the medium through which the Spirit operates to fulfill its purpose.

A Human is a Spirit while God is the Spirit. God is in us and we are in God. The mind of a Human is an extension of Universal Mind or Spirit. Human evolution is the unfolding of the Universal Mind through Human thought. The soul and Spirit are interspersed with each other and both have omnipresence.

There is something within the Human mind that desires to think of God or Spirit as a person. In each one of us, through each one of us, Spirit-God is personalized.

I AM GOD operating through this personality for the benefit of Earth, all life on the Earth and beyond.

Soul and Spirit are not separate from one another they are really two aspects of the same thing. The Soul is subjective to Spirit, receives impressions from Spirit and acts on them. Soul-Stuff refers to the primoral or undifferentiated Substance from which all things are made.

THE LAW OF NATURE

The Law of Nature, a force of nature, is a mental force, an intelligent and creative one, like electricity which can either light our house, cook our food or electrocute us if we use it incorrectly.

God reveals Itself to us, but only by revealing Itself through us

There is Creative Intelligence within the soil of Earth. It produces from the seeds placed in it. Our sub-conscious is like this same Intelligence and creates the seeds of thought we plant there. Within our sub-conscious there can be conflicting thoughts that have been stored there. This is a possible cause for our manifestation not to be immediate.

The soil and our sub-conscious are both neutral creative mediums. They are Mind in action. Soul is the medium through which all Law and Power operate. Biblically we are told "as we believe it will be done unto us." It is necessary for us to have faith, conviction and acceptance. Our belief measures the extent and degree of our blessings. We can only experience as much of life as we can embody.

The Law of Mind and Law of Attraction will bring us the type of experiences we hold in our mind and the level of abundance we believe we deserve. We do not need to sacrifice or live in poverty, or martyr ourselves in any way to please God.

Prayer does something to the mind of the one praying. It does not do anything to God. The power of prayer is in the faith and acceptance of the one praying. We must hold a mental equivalent of the thing we desire. Having a strong mental picture, concept or intention and holding to that equivalent regardless of circumstances or conditions, we will sooner or later manifest according to our concept, if it is karmically allowed. We get back what we send out in thought and feeling. Jesus said, "When you pray, believe that you have and you shall receive."

The range of possibilities always extends far beyond the range of our present concepts. There are more possibilities of how the Universe can fulfill our desires than we are capable of imagining. We can unfold our consciousness gradually to accept larger and larger concepts and greater mental equivalents. Feelings and emotions are creative. If we combine our written desires with positive emotion the Spirit of the Law begins to work. We exist in limitless opportunities which seeks expression through us.

THERE IS ONE LIFE AND THAT LIFE IS WITHIN ME NOW
THAT LIFE IS MY LIFE NOW

If we release our negative habits and thought patterns and accept thoughts of a more positive reality, the Law will begin to work in our favor. We must first trust there is a Spirit within us. Our heart beating is proof of that Spirit. Spirit is always available to us if we ask and listen for a response.

We have a tendency to get stuck sometimes in How could this possibly happen? The how is God's job. The what, the design, the matrix is our job. Instead of faith in God most people have faith in fear of loss of position, money, love or life. Faith in the invisible brings it into the visible. Faith is knowing the Universe is a spiritual knowing system and we are a part of that system. Faith is understanding the life of God is also the life in us.

Faith in the Law helps us to use our understanding of the Law with greater inward conviction.

We cannot believe any Law of the Universe will ever change its own nature, because we desire it to do so. Universal Laws are absolute. We cannot project one thing and get something else, if we do it is because in our sub-conscious, we believe something else. We can have only what we can believe. Our perceptions of life create the molds the Universe can fill. When we enlarge our consciousness we can receive more.

When we think affluently we begin to demonstrate prosperity. The first step to prosperity is gratitude for what we already have. Our dreams and wishes for health and for material things will reach no higher level than our belief in the power of God and our belief in a benevolent Universe.

All cause and effect are in Spirit bound together in one complete whole like the acorn holding the complete potential of the giant oak tree. We hold the seed of God within us. We are capable of becoming more because of this Spirit seed.

We are to see our desires as already accomplished and rest in perfect confidence, peace and certainty, never looking for results, never wondering when, never becoming anxious, never being harried nor worried. Worry stops the process of what we desire and instead gives us what the doubt and worry represent. We are to follow the intuitive suggestions of our soul and not to attempt to understand how the manifestation will occur. In my experience, it is like following bread crumbs each day, not seeing how it will lead me to my desire.

In the forty years I've worked with Spirit I've often wished for Spirit to be logical and efficient, but this has not been my experience. If I follow the bread crumbs, the soul's suggestions even though I can't see how doing the thing suggested is going to get me closer to my goal, miracles happen. Cosmic creation moves from idea to object. It does not know anything about process. Fortunately our souls see the bigger picture and sees routes that are completely invisible to us. It is useful to understand it is always about the people we will meet along the way.

Spirit's way is not about speed or a more efficient way to get something accomplished. It is helpful to enjoy the journey, the wandering.

THERE IS ONE SUPREME INTELLIGENCE THAT GOVERNS, GUIDES AND GUARDS, IT TELLS ME WHAT TO DO, WHEN AND HOW TO ACT

LAW OF ATTRACTION

We are thinking beings and we cannot stop thinking. Creative Mind receives our thoughts and cannot stop creating. What it creates depends wholly on what we are thinking. What we attract depends upon where we focus our thoughts. Every person is surrounded by this thought atmosphere. Our mental attitudes are a result of our conscious and unconscious thoughts. Through this power we are either attracting or repelling; like attracts like.

THE ESSENCE OF ALL LIFE IS GOD

By the activity of our thoughts things come into our lives. There is no power in the Universe but us that can free us. There is no messiah coming to save us. We are the messiah of our own lives.

Jesus said, "Act as if I AM and I will be there." He didn't mean He would be there; he meant our I AM Presence would be there. We are dealing with One Power that creates from Itself and we are part of that Power. It is good to think of ourselves as, "I AM one with the Source."

LAW OF REFLECTION

It is good to cultivate an attitude of friendship toward everyone and everything. We cannot receive love until we send out love vibrations. It is good to live with an attitude of, "Everyone wishes the best for me and I wish the best for everyone." I also choose to live with the attitude, "Positive exceptions are always made in my favor." I take seriously that I am an instrument of God. I feel it is reasonable to expect positive exceptions to be made in my favor and, because I expect it those exceptions are usually forth coming.

I am uplifted and surrounded by all love, all friendship, all happiness, all success and by all the support I need and desire. There is a Divine Principle and, what it does for us, it must do through us. How we expect to be treated influences others toward us.

When there is no longer anything in our mentality, which contradicts or denies our word, a demonstration will be made. It is useful to think of Law and Spirit as our friends. We should expect the best and live the best becomes our experience.

Imagination is one of our most valuable gifts. Imagination creates images and the images attract our reality. We must be specific in what we imagine, because reflection of our image is what will happen. If we imagine we will always have a parking place we will begin to prove this Law to ourselves. Everything depends on our ability to imagine, to contrive. This does not mean one must visualize. Visualizing vibrationally is Third and Fourth dimensional. To imagine is of a higher vibration than to visualize. Ignorance of the Law does not change the result. We live in Mind and It can return to us only what we believe.

SEE GOD AS YOUR SILENT PARTNER

If we normally allow the World's opinion to control our thinking, then that will be our demonstration. We can create a new pattern, not just for ourselves but for, Humanity, by projecting new patterns, especially in groups, because the energy of the group is exponentialzed by the number of people in the group. It is important to stay filled with faith, hope , love and expectancy regardless of what seems to be happening in the World. See only what you wish to experience and look at nothing else.

There can be no failure in God's Mind, and this is the Power on which we are depending. We need to realize we may be making statements, requests that our sub-conscious or unconscious mind rejects or denies. Watch for doubt or contradiction, arguments within yourself. Refuse to accept them. We are declaring the truth of the Spirit within us. An affirmation can transmute a negative thought or a previously held negative belief.

YOUR RESULT CAN ONLY BE AS PERFECT AS YOUR PATTERN

Our sub-conscious minds are the place where Universal Subjectivity and the Creative Medium Itself reacts to our personal use of it. Everyone is Universal, on the subjective side of life, and we are individual only at the point of our conscious perceptions. We use the Power of the Universal Mind every time we think. All thought is creative according to the impulse, emotion or conviction behind the thought. We do not create Laws or Principles, but we can discover and make use of them. The sub-conscious cannot analyze, dissect or deny, because of its nature it must always accept our thoughts and act on them.

ETHER IS THE CEMENT OF MATTER

No two physical particles ever touch each other, no two electrons. They are all divided from each other by space, "ether" and ether is the cement of matter.

The theory is the Laws of Attraction and Repulsion, Gravitation, Adhesion and Cohesion, operate through ether, or upon Mind, or our mind must operate through the medium of ether and the Universal Mind to create. Anything that has ever been thought at any time in the history of Humans, exists today in Universal Mind. When we meditate and connect to Universal Mind there is no past, present or future. They merge into one medium.

We can use the Law of Mind best if we understand its nature. We can demonstrate the Law or manifest only at the level of our understanding and willingness to control and focus our minds.

When we gradually increase our wisdom and understanding, and realize more Truth and apply Truth in our thoughts and actions, the more we realize positive results. It is a wonderful experience to realize we can make conscious use of the Law by planting an idea in Mind and then see it take form. We should make a mental picture of our ideal lives every day imagining only good.

We do not have to make the Law work; it is Its nature to work. We should make known our desires, and in confidence, wait upon the Law to manifest through us. Our part is to be willing to be guided by our intuition and the suggestions of our soul. There is an Intelligence within us that knows the Truth and how to make good decisions.

There is no medium between us and God, Universal Mind except our own thought that there is. The Mind we use is the same Mind of the Universe and we can have conscious access if we choose it. We live in a perfect Universe, but we must mentally see it as perfect and spiritually experience it, before it can become a part of our everyday lives. We can only have as much power as we are willing to embody.

The Spirit within us is God and only to the degree that we listen to and seek to follow this Spirit's suggestion will we really succeed. God is the Divine Presence. Law is a mechanical force like electricity anyone can use it. The highest realization we can have is the omnipresence of Spirit. Spirit is everywhere in everything. We can train our thought to recognize Spirit in everything we do, say or think.

As soon as we recognize that God is, we can turn to the Law and tell it what to do with our thoughts. We should give thanks that the Law exists and then command the Law to work. Jesus had authority because He understood His communion with Spirit. The Law is subject to Spirit. We are

Spirit, but until we accept this as truth we will only be dabbling in using the Law.

EVERY PROBLEM WE HAVE IS PRIMARILY MENTAL

When we know that we know, we can prove our knowing by doing. We need to erase from our consciousness any senses of lack by replacing it with thoughts of abundance. One thought can neutralize another thought. We must maintain a consistent, positive, aggressive mental attitude of Truth. The only reason we have felt limited is that we have not allowed our Divinity to fully express.

THE LAW OF CAUSE AND EFFECT

Karmic Law, which means the Law of Cause and Effect, works through the medium of Universal Soul, which is the Creative Principle of Nature and the Law of Spirit. Spirit and Soul are eternal. The impartial, impersonal Universal Soul is the medium through which Spirit works. It is a blind force not knowing, only doing. It was called by the ancients "maya, from which arose the teachings of the illusions of the mind, the mirror of the mind. That which is called subjective mind and the subjective mind is a place where Universal Subjectivity, the Creative Medium Itself, reacts to our personal use of It.

Within us, there is a creative field which we call subjective mind (or sub-conscious mind) and around us there is a field called universal Subjectivity. One is Universal and one is individual, but in reality they are one. There is one Mental Law in the Universe and where we use It, it becomes our law, because we have individualized It. It is impossible to plumb the depths of the individual mind, because it is not really individualized. We cannot separate ourselves from the one Mind, the Mind of God. There is no limit to the Universal Mind therefore there is endless possibility for expansion only limited by our perception.

9.

The Miracle Of Imagination

Textbooks and dictionaries seem unable to agree on any definition of imagination. The thesaurus lists over 50 synonyms. But, since all of us have imagination, each of us has first-hand knowledge of what it is and does. It seems to me there are two kinds of imagination: creative and non-creative. One runs itself, which is non-creative and includes uncontrollable and unhealthy forms such as hallucinations, delusions of grandeur, persecution complexes, inferiority complexes, martyr complexes, nightmares, fears, imagining hurts to one's feelings, hypochondria, enjoying imaginary ills and obsessive worry. These all involve the desire to run away from difficulty—to misuse one's imagination as a way to flee from reality. The other form, creative imagination, we can control and drive.

Worry is a non-creative form of imagination, all too normal and too often accepted as uncontrollable. We can change worry by substituting for destructive and fearful imaginings, positive and constructive pictures of life, its meaning and its possibilities.

Imagination is an integral part of the Human mind-body function. Never underestimate the value of ideas. Make an effort to think up a new idea every day. Doing this increases your mental acuity. Think of making imagination your hobby. Creative power can be stepped up by effort and there are ways to improve our creative thinking.

Learning institutions have slighted development of the Human creative mind in favor of filling the student's mind with facts to memorize and remember. The thinking mind is a Human's greatest gift. We have two minds, the judicial mind, which analyzes compares and chooses and the creative mind which visualizes foresees and generates ideas. Judgment has its place and keeps imagination on track. Imagination not only opens ways to action, but also can enlighten judgment.

Most of Humanity ignores their creativity assigning it to artists and inventors. Only in forced circumstances do many people attempt to try to use their creative minds.

IMAGINATION IS HUMANITY'S GREATEST GIFT

Without the use of the imagination, Humanity would still be a species living on seeds, fruit, roots and uncooked flesh. The inventing of the wheel and its many uses, the use of fire, the use of water to power, the harnessing of electricity, the creation of engines, the invention of tools, such as the hammer, the vice and the fulcrum has changed Humanity's life forever. And now the invention of radios, televisions, telephones, microwaves, x-rays, computers, the Internet, email, Facebook, web sites, cell phones, I Pads, etc. has caused us to be a truly global society. It was only about 500 years ago Europe began to rate the power of thinking, and especially creative thinking on par with the power of brute force. This new attitude was the essence of the Renaissance.

The invention of the internal combustion engine improved the farming and manufacturing industries to the extent that production put many people out of work. Imagination had to create new industries, to create new jobs.

When I think back, even in my lifetime, at all the things that have been invented I am astonished. It seems with each generation, creative, inventive progress has sped up. And now, in this Information Age, especially electronic and digital ideas and inventions are coming so fast and being developed so swiftly as to be mind boggling. Competition has forced business to recognize the importance of conscious creative effort. Many companies have hired teams of creative researchers to improve their products and their advertising.

Ideas have been, and can be, the solution to almost every Human problem. Ideas are gifted to Humanity from higher vibrational sources. The people who get quiet and listen, pay attention, receive inspiration of new ideas and if they act on those ideas they increase their abundance. The word inspiration comes from "to inspire" meaning "to be filled with Spirit." The fact that ideas are sent to the patent office, from all over the World, and must be stamped with date and time proves those that listen are receiving these ideas from higher realms and the ideas are available to anyone. To receive the solutions to the problems Humans have created for themselves, and for the Earth, it will take people who are willing to listen and to implement the ideas that are given down from higher realms.

By spending time listening, whether we do it by meditating or simply paying attention to our thoughts when we are doing repetitive actions; we can be gifted with ideas and inspiration to lift ourselves over the obstacles in our lives. The more ideas we think up, or more accurately, receive the richer and more satisfying our lives are likely to be. Worry is essentially a misuse of imagination. If we use the time and energy we usually spend worrying, in imagining creative solutions, our lives will be smoother and more enjoyable. The lack of creative effort, or the misuse of imagination, is often at the bottom of mental unrest and nervous upsets. Doing something creative will calm the nerves and improve self-esteem and self-respect.

When we don't feel well, we can cause ourselves to feel better by thinking of something worthwhile. A sense of well- being flows from having an idea and putting it into words or actions. The more we attempt to create the better we will feel. Creative work can be fun. No people enjoy their work as much as those who deal with ideas. We can get more fun out of life by making more use of our imaginations. The more creative we are, the more we will feel fulfilled as a people.

All of us have within us some Divine creative urge. Everyone has hunches. Everyone has intuition. Everyone has the ability to receive inspiration from higher dimensions. The more we intend to receive inspiration and creative ideas the more we will receive them. It takes practice to shut out negative thinking and worry and transform those habits of thought into listening to our intuition for ideas and inspiration. Then it takes courage and action to follow through with implementing the ideas we are given.

We have all been given creative talents. The degree of our talent is largely influenced by effort. It is often our drive, rather than the degree of talent, that determines our creative ability. Actual doing is the best exercise of our creative ability. The way to create is to create, just as the way to write is to write. It is a proven fact that, during war time, people make more effort to be creative. When the need arises, Humans by nature, begin to be more creative. Our imaginations seem to work harder when driven by duty, desperation, need or affection.

There is no evidence higher education induces creative power. For one thing most educational institutions ignore the subject of imagination. In America, supposedly due to lack of funding, the public schools are closing out the creative arts programs of art and music and keeping reading, writing, math and science. Many highly educated people are sterile creatively, while others accomplish outstanding results in spite of almost total lack of formal instruction.

Creative power sometimes makes up for lack of technical schooling or specialized training. The telegraph was worked out by Morse, a professional painter of portraits. The steamboat was thought up by Fulton, also an artist. Eli Whitney was a school teacher who devised the cotton gin. Irving Berlin had no musical training. It was said of him, "He can neither read music nor transcribe it – he can only give birth to it."

Higher education gives us a greater grasp on life, a more orderly way of thinking, a clearer judgment and these gains are useful to good living, but the amount of one's creative power does not depend upon a degree. Self-confidence is one of the keys to increased creativity. Imagination lasts longer than memory. We can keep our creative power, regardless of age, as long as we keep our desire. Our creative ability can keep growing year after year in pace with the effort we put into it. Imagination grows by exercise. Imagination is like muscle, if we don't use it, it will atrophy. Although older people have a tendency to lose some of their memory power, creative imagination is ageless. Fiction takes more creative power than fact.

If we allow ourselves to get in a rut, quit being curious and just stop trying, we cannot help but be less creative. Ideas often come when we are bathing, shaving, putting on makeup, driving, taking a walk, folding laundry, gardening, riding a bike, exercising, meditating, sewing, riding a bus, train, airplane, doing routine or repetitive actions. Often the best ideas come when we are falling asleep or just as we wake up. At these times our brain frequency has slowed and we are in an alpha state of consciousness, receptive to receiving higher vibrations of thought from other dimensions. We are more likely to be operating from our right brain.

Insomnia is often a sign our soul is attempting to communicate with us. Insomnia may awaken creativity. If we fear, we will not be able to sleep and worry over our wakefulness, we are more likely not to be able to fall asleep or stay asleep. If we make it a practice to pick something to think about, for which we want ideas, we can use the time of wakefulness usefully and usually our creativity will reward us with insights and ideas. Remember, don't be mad that you are having trouble falling asleep instead seek something creative to think over. If you awaken in the middle of the night and have trouble going back to sleep, rather than worry about not sleeping or worry about some situation in your life, invite your soul to give you creative inspiration. Sit up with pencil and pad and listen. Spirit muses love the middle of the night and early morning, when most activity and sound have ceased around us. When there is the least amount of activity and static in the ethers, it is easier to receive creative, inspired ideas. Do not use the time to fret. Use the time to write or to read something useful, which will usually cause you to fall asleep.

A good long shower or bath will cleanse the aura of thought forms and emotions, and clear the way for sleep, meditation or increase mental clarity for receiving creativity inspiration. Chores are also good coaxers of creative ideas, because most chores are repetitive, such as weeding, mowing the lawn, mooping, vacuuming, folding laundry, reorganizing a cabinet or drawer, ironing, doing dishes or empting the dishwasher.

Many of us travel to and from work. Travel time can be used creatively if we don't distract ourselves with radio, newspaper, doing email, playing computer games, reading or having I pod ear plugs and music going. Silence is helpful, but not essential to receiving inspired ideas. If you are driving having a recorder in your pocket or console is useful. If you take a bus, train, plane or subway the vibrations and rhythm of the vehicle can inspire ideas. Writing thoughts can be useful even if you only carry 3 by 5 cards on which to capture ideas. I've found, I'm more creative when writing by hand than typing into a computer or electronic device. There is something about the hand moving a pencil across paper that connects to the creative part of my brain. When I first started receiving information from my soul I wrote with number two lead pencils. The organic substances of wood and lead seem conducive to allowing the energy to flow through me and onto the paper. Do not try to edit what you receive until a later time.

Concentration is important. Concentration is nothing but attention, sharply focused and steadily sustained, and is an acquired habit rather than a natural gift. It does take effort, but with practice it is possible to focus one's attention even in a noisy or busy situation. Fatigue and apathy do more to kill concentration than noise or crowds.

We have reproductive imagination, which makes it possible for us to bring pictures back into our minds of things previously seen. We also have the ability to have controlled or structured visualization, which includes deliberately creating a vision of a desired object or objective. We have empathic imagination, which makes it possible to feel for others. People go to theatres, watch movies and soap operas mainly to lose themselves in the lives of others whom they see and hear. We do the same thing with reading, but reading is less passive and requires a little effort to mentally construct the scenes and actions.

The Golden Rule embodies the noblest use of empathic imagination. To "do unto others," we have to imagine how they would like to be treated, as well as know how we would like to be treated. This also holds true for choosing gifts for others.

Anticipative imagination makes it possible for us to think ahead, makes it possible for us to guess. Anticipative imagination can be used to deliberately brighten each day. We can look forward to our most pleasant part of the day ahead. We can imagine everything going our way. We can imagine positive exceptions being made in our favor. The highest form of anticipative imagination is creative expectancy. When we look forward to something we want to come true, and strongly believe it will come true, we can often make ourselves make it come true.

Creative imagination involves hunting and changing what is found. Hunting and changing are the two powers that enables a creative thinker to arrive at new ideas. We can find something that is not really new, but is new to us. There is a difference between discovery and invention. We can discover something as Newton did gravity and as Franklin did electricity, but the inventive imagination comes into play when the discoverer chooses to use the discovery in a creative manner. Think of all the ways the association of ideas has used both of these discoveries. A person can discover light can also be used for heat. Imagination can bring together those things or thoughts which are not new in and of themselves, but can be cooked up into that which is new. This happens every day especially in the creation of new recipes.

Creativity is more than mere imagination. It is imagination inseparably coupled with both intent and effort. Creative imagination may be thought of as the action of mind which produces a new idea or insight. What sparks the spark? We have not yet learned what makes the heart beat. Creative imagination is just as mystic or more so. It is an evidence of divinity. There is at work, in the World, an influence which may be described as creative. It is capable of reinforcing life and enhancing natural faculty.

Creativity requires forward thinking. Creative imagination uses the material of previous experience to produce something new rather than reproducing the past. The knowledge and experiences we have tucked away in our mind are indispensable. Imagination, like reason, cannot run without the fuel of knowledge, but constant awareness is essential. First-hand experience provides the richest fuel for creative power. Second-hand experience—such as superficial reading, listening, or spectating—gives us far thinner fuel. Prosperity often tends to impoverish us creatively, whereas hard going or struggle tends to call forth our creativity. Travel is another rich source of creative inspiration.

Remaining alert and continuing our self-education steps up our creative power. Self-education causes us to observe as many worthwhile facts as possible. It is important to remember what we have observed and to combine the facts to come to creative conclusions. The effort we put into self-education pays off in added creative power.

In observing today's children I wonder if we are doing them a disservice. Most of the things they are exposed to murder wonder. Most children are not exposed in creative ways to nature. For the most part their play, sports, and education are so regimented as to remove curiosity and wonder.

Association plays a big part in the accidental factor of creativity. The association of ideas is what gears imagination to memory and causes one thought to lead to another. The ancient Greeks stated as the Three Laws of Association: contiguity, similarity, and contrast. By contiguity they meant nearness, as when a baby's shoe reminds you of an infant. By similarity they meant a picture of a lion will remind you of your cat. By contrast they meant a midget might remind you of a giant. There is also the Law of Cause and Effect, which means a yawn may remind you it is time to retire. Association can be enriched by selective attention. Association can also work through sounds or smells rather than words. Smells can invoke chains of thought and are one of our strongest forms of remembered associations.

Our power of association will produce more ideas if we keep a notebook and jot down our hunches, our observations and our conclusions. Ideas are flighty things and are often as hard to remember as our dreams. Although many of your ideas may not work out, there is a good chance they may suggest other thoughts. I keep 3 by 5 cards beside where I read and keep a small notebook in my purse and a recorder in my car for this purpose. Check lists, note pads, purposely being positive, stick- to-it-tiveness can all cause our power of association to well up more ideas for us out of the storage in our memory.

Many people believe combination is the essence of creativity, a creative thinker evolves no new ideas; they actually evolve new combinations of ideas that are already in their mind. One of the richest men in Oklahoma saw a box sitting atop a folding chair. His mind took the image farther and put wheels on the chair and invented the grocery cart. As a child, Pasteur had a memory of neighbors being poisoned and driven crazy by bites from a rabid wolf. Pasture created many man-guarding vaccines, but he was most driven to find a vaccine to cure the victims of rabies, because of the dreadful childhood memory.

Creative thinking is not purely an intellectual process; the thinker is dominated by their emotions and their will. Emotional drive is self-starting and largely automatic, whether based on hunger, fear, love or ambition. The other kind of energy depends upon determination rather than feelings, and has to be cranked.

Every brain has a section that can create ideas. It is called the "silent area" since it controls no body-movement and has nothing to do with what we see or hear or physically feel. It is a lump of tissue called the thalamus. In this lobe, our basic emotions are centered. It is known ideas flow faster under emotional stress. When in a jam our imaginations often soar. The emotional lobe is wired, by nerves, to the frontal area in such a way as to affect creative thinking.

Fright is too treacherous a drive, because it is an animal urge that throws us back to where we were before our intellects developed. Fright is akin to fear of punishment. Fear of punishment may make us work hard physically, but a person cannot focus their creative mind when obsessed by fear of punishment. Even the slightest degree of coercion tends to cramp imagination. Dictators and totalitarian rulers work hard to keep fear alive in the people they rule. They are aware that freedom will cause creative thinking and revolt.

Love and patriotism are better driving powers. Love of country inspired hundreds of thousands of our people to think up ideas that helped to win the first and second World Wars. Hard going induces hard effort in the nation as well as in the individual. Creative effort in times of prosperity has tended to ebb, whereas depressions have brought about extra efforts that have resulted in much advancement.

Love makes the average woman unceasingly think up things for her family. Maternal drive generates far more ingenious effort than thirst, hunger or sex. Love when turned to hate can lift a non-creative person to creative heights. Many criminals are highly creative, but choose to use their creativity in non- productive ways.

Fear of poverty is an even stronger urge than the hope for wealth. The Spirit of intellectual adventure, vanity, and the desire for self-realization can be motivators. Lack of childhood security fuels some people to excel. It has spurred me into a habit of effort I don't think I would possess if I had been raised with a sense of security. Being raised in lower economic circumstances caused me to develop a habit of creative effort, making something better from what was available in front of me. I acquired a master's degree in "making do." I've never been particularly motivated by deadlines, but deadlines put some people into a hyper creative mode.

Some people can start themselves thinking creatively by asking themselves questions: "What can I do to get ahead in my job? What can I do to make this party, this relationship a success?"

Most people fear attempting to be creative because of fear of judgment, their own and the fear of their creation being judged by others. Creative thinking calls for a hopeful, positive, enthusiastic attitude, which can be easily quashed by the critical judgment of others. It is good to not let anyone read, see or be aware of your creativity until you have completed it to your own satisfaction. Premature judgment can stop the flow of creativity. It is important to not let our own inner critic sap our creative ideas and efforts. We need self-encouragement to be creative. We also need to be self-disciplined in order to not abandon our own ingenuity. Our need to conform often stifles our creativity. Praise tends to make creativity bloom, while judgment, discouragement, wisecracks and criticism kills it.

Perfectionism kills creativity. Many artists are jealous and many art teachers are not supportive of young talent, because they fear being out done. Be careful in choosing a teacher, who is strong enough in their own creativity, to not be threatened by the talent of others. Choose teachers who are encouraging and supportive. Often we did not have a choice in teachers while we were in school and teachers have the power to demolish a person's self-confidence in their creative ability. I let myself be stopped artistically in the third grade and didn't begin again until after I was forty due to the judgment of one teacher. Everyone needs encouragement to be creative.

Creative people succeed because they begin, they try, they attempt, they experiment, and they just keep trying. Too many people fear even attempting to be creative, by comparing themselves to others, they feel are extremely gifted creatively. We never know what we are capable of creatively until we attempt and don't give up after the first attempt but stick to it and discipline ourselves to show up regularly with materials that can spark creativity. The trouble with the average person is that they do not sufficiently trust themselves to create and to deliver ideas. The more creative thinking and action we do, and the more ideas we express, the more competent we become, and with creative effort comes a most satisfying sense of accomplishment.

Make the goal of cherishing your experience more important than the goal of getting somewhere Spirituality and creativity exist in different dimensions than ordinary time.

Whatever it is you desire you must become this in your mind, words, feelings, desires, and actions. Act as if, and you are. The outer must correspond to the inner.

There are two kinds of action, required action and inspired action. Required action would be to gain the necessary education and internship if you desire to be a doctor. Inspired action, on the other hand comes from inner spiritual urges that spark one's passion to take immediate action on them.

Often when we begin to practice the art of manifestation, or anything else, we will reach a plateau where it seems as if nothing else is happening. This plateau often causes people to quit or give up, but if we continue to practice we find life happens in peaks and valleys. You never know how your practice/efforts/actions will produce results. Anyone can commit to do anything for a minute. Life is only lived one minute at a time. Mastering anything requires patience.

Do whatever you are doing 100 percent, regardless of how small or insignificant it may seem at the time. Give it your best. Experience a sense of joy in whatever your present activity, regardless of how mundane. Notice the sensual feel of water on your hands when you wash dishes or the fresh smell of clean sheets as you make your bed or fold the laundry. By paying attention to the colors, the textures and sounds, the tastes, and the smells, you experience present moment connectedness with everything. This attention heightens your awareness of being present and enriches your life. The core work of living a Humanly successful and divinely spiritual life is to stay present no matter what you are doing.

It is not what we teach that is most learned—it is what we are.

It is far easier to teach Truth than to practice It, but the practice is the teaching. We are surrounded by an all-pervasive Spirit of God. That Spirit is the creator of life and the World and that Spirit is within us.

We may not feel we are in control of all of the events of our lives, but we are or can be in control of how we respond to them. Learning to choose our responses. to the outer and merging our will of self with the will of God, is the ultimate goal to a happy and successful life.

When we learn to trust our instincts, our intuition, and the multidimensional timing of things we step into lives that are more expansive and sweeter than anything we have imagined. I often say, "Thy will be done and follow it by, but could you hurry?" I've found that Spirit's attention and the feeling of being loved, heard and cherished, by my soul, has fulfilled much of my longing to have these things from other people.

The only thing that matters is following your truth.

Make the goal of cherishing your experience more important than the goal of getting somewhere. Practice allowing yourself to do what you can do, when you can do it. If you didn't do something yesterday, do it today. If you can't do it right now, do it in an hour. If you can't do all of it, do some of it.

If I choose, there is nothing in my thought about the past, that can in any way deny me the pleasure and privilege of living today as though everything was complete and perfect.

When I focus on my expectation, instead of what IS happening, I miss the opportunity to be happy.

The culture of constant productivity actually makes us less productive, because it distracts us from our surroundings and the sense of oneness we can experience when we pay attention to where we are. It heightens our anxiety, because there is always one new message to be answered, one new thing to do.

Practicing a Namaste attitude by approaching people with compassion and an awareness of their divinity can be a challenging but transformative spiritual practice.

10.

Belief, Faith, Knowingness

We can know something because we have read it or heard it from our elders. Most of our beliefs have been handed down to us from others. Some of these people we have considered to be authorities and we've taken their word, for what is true, without checking it out for ourselves. When we first start questioning, if we ever do, we begin to wonder: Who am I really? Am I what other people have told me? Am I the roles I play?

We are not our names. We are not our bodies. We are not our minds. We are not our occupations. We are not our relationships. We are not our country, race or religion. We are the intangible, invisible, indestructible spiritual Self having these experiences. We are consciousness.

I learned this lesson in 1979. I lost all the roles I was playing up to that point in a nine-month period. I found myself in a strange place, alone and without any roles. I sat with a legal pad on my lap and I tried to figure out who I was without a husband, parents, lover, children, a job, friends, family or even being a member of the Episcopal Church. I wrote I AM, and in the space after I just couldn't seem to figure out what I was without the roles I was used to playing. I did wonder, since I was no longer playing roles, who was inside me even asking this question? I ended up with a whole column of I AM. Of course, at the time, I didn't know that was the answer; that before and after everything else, we are the I AM, the Spirit having the Human experience. I didn't understand or learn this for another three years until I began to have direct communication with my soul.

Wayne Dyer in his book, *Your Sacred Self*, says there are ten most common and difficult-to-undo beliefs we have been taught in Western civilization.

MORE IS BETTER – This belief locks us into striving and never really arriving or enjoying life. To undo this belief, it is important to simplify our lives and to look at what we are attempting to fill within ourselves by striving to have more and more and more.

EXTERNALS ARE TO BLAME FOR THE CONDITIONS OF MY LIFE – We are taught to blame the weather, our parents, the culture, politicians, luck and even illness or heredity or the flu season. To undo this belief and stop blaming, we must eventually accept total responsibility for our thoughts and actions.

IDEALISM CAN'T COEXIST WITH REALISM – We are taught only what we can see is real. In actuality, nothing is real and nothing is imagined. Everything is perception. To undo this belief, we will need to learn to rely on our wisdom mind rather than our ordinary, judgmental mind. We must learn to trust our intuition rather than what appears to be happening or what other people tell us.

THERE IS ONLY ONE EXISTENCE AND IT IS PHYSICAL – We are brought up to believe we are our bodies and only what is physical is real. To undo this belief, it is important to develop an awareness of the observer within ourselves, the one observing the actions and thoughts of the physical being. It is useful to make ourselves available to non- physical realities.

WE ARE SEPARATE AND DISTINCT FROM EVERYONE ELSE – Our education emphasizes believing in sensory experiences. These experiences seem to tell us we are separate, unique, and special, disconnected from each other and the Earth. We learn from physicists we are all made from the same substance and so is the Earth. We are only separate in our perception. In actuality, everything is made of one unifying substance.

THERE IS AN "US" VERSUS A "THEM" – We live in a civilization that thrives on this concept and labels and divides families, nationalities, races and members of different political and religious beliefs. In order to overcome this belief, it is useful to begin to think of ourselves as Universal Humans or at least Global Humans, Planetary Citizens, or Earthlings rather than members of a select group.

PETTY TYRANTS SHOULD BE IGNORED – There are bad people in the

World and they should be avoided and ignored. In order to overcome this belief, we must reach a point of being able to witness the Spirit within each person. We may not be comfortable with or approve of their behavior, but at their core they are also spiritual beings. We learn from these people how not to be victims. Everything that comes into our lives is for the purpose of teaching us.

GOALS ARE ESSENTIAL FOR SUCCESS – It is important to have goals and to be aware of our purpose, but also to be flexible in our pursuits. To overcome the belief we must have goals, and not deviate from their pursuit, it is important to understand that our purpose is to seek guidance from our soul to understand our true purpose in being here, which is expansion. Then to follow what we believe is our purpose and our personal goals with enthusiasm and vigor and trust the Universe is willing to assist us to become all we are capable of becoming.

YOU MUST ALWAYS DO YOUR BEST – Your best leaves no room for improvement. It means you have to give 100 per cent at all times. Continually doing your best involves enormous stress and pressure. Usually you are measuring yourself against someone else's standards. To overcome this belief, it is important to receive guidance and to follow that guidance to the best of our ability and to not compare ourselves or our performance to that of others. It is important, at the level of our souls, we not be competitive, but we be creative.

DREAMS ARE NOT REALITY – We are taught there are two separate realities. One is our waking reality; the other is our dream reality. To overcome this belief, we would do well to understand our dreams and our waking reality are created by the same brain and these separate energy experiences are interrelated. Again, the most important thing is to cultivate the witness within ourselves that watches both realities.

We are all enrolled in the school of Earth. We chose much of our curriculum before we chose to embody for this incarnation. Blaming what is happening with us on something outside ourselves doesn't serve our spiritual growth.

Beliefs are handed to us. Knowing comes from within. No one can hand you knowing. You can believe a thing, but still have doubt; once you have the experience that proves or disproves the belief, then you can have knowing. When you have direct experience in your own life, it is easier to give up doubt.

I had believed in Jesus on the word of religious authorities, but doubted much of what was written in the *Bible*. On two separate occasions in my life, the Master Jesus has materialized in front of me and we have had direct conversations. This definitely moved believing in Him and knowing Him into my reality. I could still doubt myself if I chose and dismiss these experiences as my imagination, but once the knowingness is instilled within me as experience I don't choose to doubt.

I had no belief in the Spiritual Hierarchy. I'd never heard of them within the context of my Christian education. When the Masters began to appear to me and converse with me to explain the workings of the Universe, even though I argued that I didn't think running the Universe as a corporation was a good idea, I became more than a believer. I now know how the Universe and galaxy operate and what positions are held by what Masters.

I had no belief in extraterrestrials, nor did I desire one, until the Federation brought ships in for me to see them and began their telepathic communication with me to explain my role in the Federation. I am a person who needs personal experience to support what I think I know. I am not a person who is able to operate with blind faith, as was encouraged when I was in the Christian churches.

Now I've developed my ability to know, through direct communication, I still depend on my intuition. Intuition is something we all have. Many people are afraid to trust their intuition and will even deny having it. Agreeing to have knowingness is a big step in our spiritual growth because it removes our excuses. Once we have knowingness, we can no longer pretend not to know, or honestly use the terms, "Well, I just don't know" or "I'm so confused." I don't personally see the value in believing things just because someone wrote them down or puts them in a newspaper, on TV or on the Internet. I think our most valuable asset as spiritual beings is the spiritual gift of discernment.

I have found it much easier to have faith, once I began to demand proof of the Universe. The Universe, our souls, the Masters are all a part of a much larger consciousness. We all have the ability to communicate with this consciousness. What stops us? Fear, feelings of unworthiness? Once we shut down our inner chatter and go into silence, we will find our witness, our soul, our God Self, whatever you want to call it. Our first step is to begin to witness our thoughts, then to look at who is witnessing the thoughts and then to follow that part of us, which is our soul. The soul does not make demands. It makes suggestions. We always have Freewill to argue, disagree or make conditions under which we will do what the soul suggests. We are not pawns. We are here to be co-creators with our souls.

Self-realization is the only authentic freedom. Authentic freedom is knowing who you are, why you are here, your purpose in life and where you are going when you leave here. It is knowing your identity is not located in the physical World but in the eternal, changeless World of God. Authentic freedom comes from knowing, not from belief.

We can only have higher awareness by asking for it and seeking it, through silence. Many people are afraid of silence. They are afraid of what the soul will ask of them. Higher awareness demands a new agreement with reality. We can doubt or we can ask and listen. We can make an effort to shut down our inner dialogue, the babblings of our ego, and listen to the voice of our soul. We can cultivate the witness. Allowing the higher self to surface, as the dominant force in our lives, will bring the only lasting peace. Doing this, we can know God on an experiential level.

The first few times I meditated with the intention and desire to hear God, I was not able to shut down my ego thoughts, but I was determined. I listened to what the ego was saying, "This is the dumbest thing you've ever done, this is not going to work. Who are you to think God would speak to you. For God's sake, put the phone back on the hook, and go get a job." I just kept sitting there with the willingness and intention to hear God, and suddenly on the right side of my brain there were other words, other than the ranting of my ego. One did not shut up when the other began to impress words into my mind. There was never a voice. It was always just words. I wrote the words and later went back and read the words. I must admit I was expecting a voice. I later learned seeing is in the vibration of the Third and Fourth dimension; hearing is in the Third, Fourth and the lowest part of the Fifth dimension; and above that, energetically, there is knowingness. My soul had not agreed to let me see or hear as I had previously requested. They were waiting for me to agree to have knowingness.

Most of the people, who are awake at this time, came to Earth from higher vibrations than seeing and hearing. If you haven't been able to hear or see spiritually, I invite you to agree to "know," to ask your soul for knowingness. Your soul would not want you to reduce your vibration lower than the one you came in with. That would be like letting you go back to kindergarten. Start where you are now, without fear of what you will be given. You can always argue, refuse or make conditions under which you will attempt what the soul is suggesting. These conditions need to be in writing, because we are operating in the Fourth dimension now. The rules of the Fourth dimension demand, to have a contract with our soul which allows the soul to intervene on our behalf; we must put our desires in writing.

Don't take what I've said as your belief; try it for yourself. From your own experience, you will develop faith, based on your own knowingness and experience, rather than following someone else's beliefs. I can assure you higher awareness demands a new agreement with reality, but it also brings peace and serenity.

Every belief you chose to call your own was the best option you had available to you at the time. You are always free to choose again.

Every experience in life is a lesson nudging us to wake up and to explore our potential. Making sense of the World is not as important a being happy. This World was designed not to make sense, but to foster growth.

11.

Intuition

TRUST YOUR GUT – CHANGE YOUR LIFE

Everyone has intuition at their disposal. It is built into the Human system. The intuition is always there. Listening to intuition, has to be a choice and it can be practiced to the extent it will protect us and lead us in the right direction for our lives. Your intuition is the wisest adviser you'll ever have. It can lead you toward what you should do and lead you away from what is not in your best interest. It is not always easy to hear your intuition or inner voice, because the voice of your ego is louder, pushier and seemingly more logical than your intuition. The constant chatter of our ego keeps a din of noise going in our heads, to attempt to keep us distracted from our intuition, the voice of our soul.

Our intuition is the body's radar, helping us to make decisions, if we are willing to pay attention. When you meet a person, you have a sub-conscious feeling: You like them or not. You trust them or you don't. We seldom stop to think, "Where does that come from?" Intuition is knowing without knowing; it's instinctively knowing something you don't know how you know. There are times when you get a feeling about something—say, I don't want to get on this flight—and you wonder: Is it my anxiety, or is it real? It's difficult to know what's fact or fiction. You can only judge over a period of time. You have to gain confidence, in your ability, to pay attention to that feeling, not the voice of the frightened ego.

Indecision and confusion are two of the worst things in life. It plagues everybody. But confusion is sometimes a blessing, when it stops you from making a move, because sometimes you're not supposed to make a move.

Wait for clarity. Confusion can be a kind of intuition; your body's way of saying, don't do anything right now—just go with the flow and the answer will come.

The most important thing is to trust your gut feeling, the first feeling you feel about something, because that very first feeling is usually the right one. Some people think of intuition as a mystical power. Skeptics write it off as a matter of lucky guesswork. But scientists, who study the phenomenon, say it's a very real ability that can be identified in lab experiments and visualized on brain scans. Research shows our instincts often hit us first on a visceral level, telling us what we need to know well, before our consciousness catches up.

Martha Beck, who writes for O Magazine, has named the two voices in her head; the ego voice, who dresses to impress, she calls Fang; her soul voice, her intuition, she calls Buddy. Buddy dresses in shorts and a tank top. I have two voices. My ego voice I call Miss Manners. She always wants me to do the things that would be acceptable to others. What she calls the "right" way to do things. My soul voice I have named Matthew. I met Matthew face to face, so to speak, in 1982 at a low point in my life when I was ready to give up my life, but instead gave it over to my soul. Since that time, Matthew and I have become good friends and he's the one person I know I can believe and trust. I'm not saying that's easy, because Matthew and, as far as I can tell, God doesn't operate with logic, at least any form of logic I've been taught or recognize. The system of the soul, the intuition, operates more with feelings, nudges, flashes, songs and images than it does with words.

I often accuse Matthew, the part of my soul I call my gatekeeper, of not understanding how things are done here on Earth. He ignores that complaint and doesn't even say, "Yes, but." He has some interest in appearance, but only to the extent it causes me to stand out in a crowd; not wearing Birkenstocks and flowing skirts, but dressing in unique ways and wearing lots of purple. He's not much interested in caution and likes for me to take lots of chances; not with my physical body, but with doing things in an unorthodox method and taking me places before he bothers to tell me why we are showing up there at a particular time. The interesting thing about following his suggestions, and he does assure me they are only suggestions, is he seems to always be right. When I follow the impulses I receive from him, I always seem to be at the right place at the right time and have remembered to take whatever might be needed with me.

It isn't that I hear a voice. It's like knowingness, a feeling, a sense.

Following these feelings, I go to certain stores, not necessarily where my logic would take me, and what I'm seeking (or what is seeking me) will be on sale. I arrive at the post office just in time to open the door for someone whose arms are loaded with packages. I miss being involved in an auto accident that has just happened. I meet someone who needs to know the name of the shampoo, to use after chemo, to get my hair to grow back thicker. I'm at the counter when a person asks the clerk for an item they don't have, but I just saw it in the previous store I was in and can let them know where to go to find the item. Matthew likes me to speak to people in public who I don't know, which is not easy for me. He encourages me to compliment people I encounter in public.

When I wonder about making a decision, I hold the choices in my mind and feel the possible outcome of each choice and how it feels in my body, as I think about each option. The emotional centers of the brain, along with the elaborate bundle of nerves in our belly (the so-called gut brain), have been evolving far longer than language. That system, more than logic, is attuned to helping us navigate our way through life.

If I have a choice to make about going somewhere on a trip, or even to a party, I project myself into the future and see if it feels like I show up there. If I can't sense myself being there, I don't make a plan to go. The Miss Manners' voice always wants me to do the expected, the right thing. I have to get quiet to hear my Matthew suggestions; he never shouts. Miss Manners shouts fear and paranoia. Matthew nudges me to risk doing new things; to extend myself beyond where I'm comfortable. Miss Manners likes to stay comfortable and safe.

Miss Manners never shuts up. She's like a neighbor who plays their TV loud and never turns it off. Sometimes I have to take a few deep breaths, take the control away from her and push the pause button to move away from the inner noise to get to the place where I can feel, what's the next thing for me to do to stay in a state of grace? If I waited for her to shut up from giving me her opinions, I would never be aware of Matthew's guidance. It just wouldn't happen.

I'm most aware of my soul voice, just before I fall asleep and just as I'm waking up. I've learned that at these times my brain waves have slowed down to about 10 cycles per second, which puts me in an alpha state of consciousness. Sometimes I can deliberately cause my brain to do this just through intention and breathing. I can deliberately go into meditation and get quiet and make the connection, but I've found I desire to have access to Matthew's opinions and suggestions 24/7 so I've practiced and intended to have it available all the time. I did meditation for years to develop this ability. I later learned that repeated meditation creates an activation of an area of the brain that makes receiving subtle information easier. We are so used to depending on our sense of sight and believing what we see, that it takes practice to see beyond the visual to the energy of what's real.

Miss Manners is always in a hurry and always wanting to prove herself right. She's always afraid of judgment from other people. Matthew is only interested in peace, calmness and connections with people. He likes me to take naps, to read certain books and to spend time in nature. Intuition, wisdom, doesn't force itself on us. It has to be desired, sought and culti-vated, to be trusted and accurate. I've found intuition is like a muscle. If I use it, if I expect it to be there, it will be. The more I depend on it, follow it, the stronger it has become.

A few years ago, people began to wear bracelets and have stickers with WWJD on them indicating, "What would Jesus do?" I use WWMS, which stands for, "What would Matthew suggest?" I've learned we never lose our Freewill just because we are willing to listen to the suggestions of our soul, our intuition. I can always say "No" or ignore my intuition and believe my logic knows more than my soul, but, trust me, I also pay the price. The soul might not be logical, but it does always have my highest good in mine.

You may need to pay attention, when you are doing a repetitive act, such as showering, putting on makeup, shaving, driving, pulling weeds, mowing the grass, doing dishes, folding laundry, walking, jogging, because repetitive action puts us in the alpha state. I watch so many people avoid silence with radio, mp3 players, computer games, email, cell phones, texting and television. It is as if Humans are afraid of silence, afraid of what they might hear in the silence. Trust me, making a space in your brain, for silence in order to contact your intuition, is the sanest and safest thing you can do.

If you want to meditate to receive information from your soul, your intuition, make sure you do a meditation that takes you only to the alpha level. Your normal thought process, where the ego is chattering, is at the beta level of brain wave. Slowing your brain wave level down to alpha is the first level beyond beta. If you become more relaxed than that, you slow the frequency to theta. It is more difficult to bring information back from theta and very easy to drop from there into delta, which is the sleep state. It takes practice to meditate and remain in alpha. My soul suggested I take a course called *The Silva Method* after they pointed me to the book in an airport gift shop. This course teaches you how to reach the alpha level and to remain there for reprogramming of your mind and to send energy to other people for the purpose of healing. If there is not a Silva Method teacher in your area, the class is available on CD's from their web site.

When I first made contact with my soul, I could only receive insight when I was in meditation; but, after attending the *Silva Method*, I had access constantly no matter what other activity was going on.

One of the methods, suggested in the Silva training, is to take a glass of water to bed with you and, before going to sleep, project into the water any question you have. Drink half the glass of water and put the other on your nightstand. Upon awakening, the next morning, drink the other half of the glass of water and mentally state you will have the answer to your question within twenty-four hours. This method puts every cell of your body on notice to become aware of the answer. It also puts your soul, your intuition, on notice to search for the answer. During the twenty-four hour period the answer may come from your intuition, from another person, from a TV or radio, from a billboard, from any avenue the intuition chooses. Our job is to remain conscious and attentive.

Your ego feels it is its job to keep fearful thoughts and images in your mind. It is our job to deliberately place positive thoughts and images into our minds through affirmations, if that works for you, or by watching our thoughts and replacing negative thoughts as they appear in our minds by saying "cancel, cancel, cancel" and reframing the negative thought. I keep positive quotes in front of me in my journal, with plaques on the wall and by reading positive material every day. I have vision boards with pictures of things I desire to have and to experience. It is our job, our responsibility, to replace the negative, fearful thoughts and images projected by our ego with positive, hopeful, cheerful images and thoughts.

Miss Manners is bossy, self-righteous and loud. I attempt to stay conscious enough to be aware of what she's feeding me in order to let Matthew's suggestions calm her down so I can proceed, in a creative way, without being stopped or influenced by her fear and indecision so strongly I stop and don't make the progress the soul desires for this body.

Martha Beck suggests we take ten minutes to write a description of our lives—stream of consciousness, no self-judgment, no editing. Then go over our description, looking for every word that carries frightening or painful associations. These words have more power than you might think. Studies show after focusing on words having to do with aging, people walk more slowly; when they see words associated with anger, they are more likely to be rude.

According to Martha, this phenomenon is called affective priming, but it works both ways. You can use it to connect with your inner wisdom by changing every stressful word, in your self-description, to something more freeing, relaxing or exhilarating. If you wrote, "I'm nervous," see whether "I'm excited" may also fit. The physiological reaction to fear and excitement are the same. The word *unsure* could be replaced by *open*. As you change your story, your ego voice will begin to soften, and the peace that comes from your wiser inner voice will begin to arise.

Most of our problems stem from lack of awareness. I found the following mental picture enlightening:

Suppose you were given a one-man airplane to use in any way you like. But you did not understand the powers of an airplane; you were unaware it could carry you across the sky. But still, wanting to make some use of it, you hitched it to a horse and drove it around. Because of your limited awareness of its use, your actual use was also limited. But after studying the machine for awhile, you discover its motor, propeller, and other items of power. So you unhitch the horse and drive the airplane around on the ground with its own power. This is an advanced use, but still far from making the most of its intended purpose, so you study some more and you discover that the airplane has wings for a practical purpose; you see the possibilities of rising above the Earth to soar aloft. With this new knowledge, you go into action. Finally, you fly. By discovering the full capacities of that airplane, it carries you to whatever destination you desire.

The Human mind is like that. The power is there all right, blocked only by our lack of awareness that it is available. We have been fighting life with the inadequate weapons of habitual, conditioned and shallow thoughts. There is a vast difference between thought and awareness. Thought is our memory in action. Thought is mere repetition. Our thoughts are based on our conditioning during our early years. Thinking is based on acquired viewpoints and attitudes which may not be in line with reality. Awareness is a revelation of the truth about something. Thought is both good and necessary for the mechanical processes of life, like building a house or cooking dinner. When we drop our conditioned opinions, we make room for the truth. Our Spiritual Self is not mechanical; it must be elevated by an entirely different power. That power is awareness. Self-awareness enables us to reject negative emotions the moment they try to sneak in.

Our intuition is our salvation. Think about the following story:

Picture a man lost in the woods. Dusk is descending and the dangers of the dark creep in. The man knows a false step might drop him into a deep pit or treacherous marsh. Wild animals lurk in the shadows. A storm threatens.

Suddenly, the lost man sights another struggling wanderer. He asks for the way out. The stranger offers immediate and friendly help. After following the stranger for a while, the lost man realizes his supposed guide is just as lost as he is. So he parts company, to set out once more on his own. Soon, he comes across a second stranger, who confidently claims to possess an accurate map of the escape route. The lost man follows this new counselor, but again it becomes obvious the man is self-deceived and his map is a pathetic result of his self-deception. The lost man wanders on in deepening despair. He runs into others, who claim knowledge of the way out, but he sees from the half- concealed distress in their eyes they are just as lost as he.

Then, as he stumbles about, the wanderer places his hand into his coat pocket for warmth. His fingers curl around something hard and reas-suring. He withdraws a compass. He laughs with comfort and relief as he realizes that it was there all along. He had only to look within himself. He had been so busy inquiring of others, that he failed to do the one necessary thing. But now he remembers to ask his soul. He remembers his intuition is always there.

Your True Self always knows just what to do and what not to do. The True Self knows the answer to every problem. When we are inwardly quiet, when we are ready to receive, it speaks. It cannot talk while we are talking. One of the best procedures, for clearing confusion, is to see plainly what doesn't work. One course that has never worked, and never will work, is distraction. Distraction is anything that prevents us from looking at the problem in the face with a mind made up to locate the solution. Our most common form of distraction is noise. Trying to solve our problems by dis-tracting ourselves with noise is like trying to untangle traffic by honking the horn. What works is quiet, relaxed receptivity.

Attempting to alter outside conditions is only temporary; changing our inner beliefs and attitudes is the only thing that brings lasting positive change.

Knowledge is the observation of a fact. Knowing is the inward experience of that fact.

The genuine purpose of our lives is the inward experiencing of the Truth itself. We can only discern the Truth through our own intuition and discernment.

One of our causes of great disappointment is unrealistic expectations of other people. The truth is, people always behave the way they are, not according to our wishes. When we attempt to change people, we may believe it is because we know what is best for them, but if we check ourselves, through self-awareness, we will usually find we have a personal agenda of why we would prefer that they would behave differently.

No person and no condition really has the power to make us feel bad. The false reaction of our mind is what makes us feel bad. Feeling bad is a choice. But we can learn to react in an entirely new way. We can withdraw the false power from people and circumstances. Then we are inwardly free from feeling bad about anything. How we feel is up to us. All feeling is a choice, based on a belief. Thought comes before emotion.

Other Books by bj King

Pentimento: Diary of a Walk-In

Self-Mastery Of Mind And Emotion

Who Are You And What On Earth Are You

Life After Life

Old Loves Are Seldom Finished ... When New Loves Begin

I Am Presence and Violet Flame

The Universal Laws and Jesus' Meaning of The Beatitudes

Manual for Spiritual Maturity

The Master Jesus Speaks

Life is A Spiritual Game

Principles of Truth

www.ingramcontent.com/pod-product-compliance
Lightning Source LLC
Chambersburg PA
CBHW021344090426
42742CB00008B/738